THE ORGANIC
WAY TO MULCHING

THE ORGANIC
WAY TO MULCHING

by the Editors of
ORGANIC GARDENING and FARMING

ROBERT RODALE, *Editor*
JEROME OLDS, *Executive Editor*
M. C. GOLDMAN, *Managing Editor*
MAURICE FRANZ, *Managing Editor*

Compilation Supervised by
GLENN F. JOHNS

The paper in this book has been made from waste paper that normally winds up at the city dump. This reclaimed paper is an example of how today's wastes can be converted into a worthwhile resource, thereby helping to solve the solid waste disposal crisis and preserving the quality of our environment.

RODALE PRESS, INC.   Emmaus, Pa.

Standard Book Number 0–87857–009–8

Library of Congress Catalog Card Number 70–170280
Copyright 1971 by Rodale Press, Inc.
All Rights Reserved
Printed in the United States

OB-702

Fourth Printing – June, 1976

CONTENTS

Introduction: There's More To Mulch Than Meets The Eye! . . .

CHAPTER

INTRODUCTION

There's More To Mulch Than Meets The Eye!

Mulch is a layer of material, preferably organic material, that is placed on the soil surface to conserve moisture, hold down weeds, and ultimately improve soil structure and fertility.

There's more to mulch than meets the eye. Be it a fluffy blanket of hay, a rich brown carpet of cocoa bean shells, or a mantle of sawdust, that "topping" for the vegetable patch and flower bed serves as much more than frosting on the garden cake.

Mulch acts. It performs in several wondrous ways. It fills a role as protector of the topsoil, conserver of moisture, guardian against weather extremes and comfortable, bruise-saving cushioner under ripening produce. It prevents weed growth while enriching the soil and all but eliminates a lot of those time-consuming, back-aching jobs like plowing and cultivating always considered necessary for a productive garden.

Another important advantage of mulching is regulating the temperature of the soil. The mulch tends to be an insulator, which means that during many periods of the year it moderates the temperature of the soil beneath. In winter a mulched soil can be warmer than other ground, and in summer it can be cooler.

Mulching around trees prevents competition by grass for moisture and nutrients. Trees, and in fact most plants, need a tremendous amount of moisture during hot weather, especially. If grass and other plants are growing right up to the trunk, they will take the moisture first and leave less for the tree. Mulching is the easiest and most attractive way for the average gardener to keep that from happening.

If you're serious about your garden, you've long ago thrown away your bags of commercial fertilizer and have started to build real productivity into your soil. And the fertility of your soil depends upon how you're able to get humus into it. That's really what mulching is all about.

Most mulching benefits can be obtained by any kind of ground cover—even the plastic sheets which are such a detriment to the welfare of our environment. But when it comes to improving the soil, nothing can do it like an organic mulch—not aluminum foil, not plastic, not polyethylene film. Organic mulches have a plus— they decompose into the essential life-giving elements of a rich, dark humus.

Plants themselves literally demand to be mulched because that's the way they've been able to survive repeated disasters through the ages. Spontaneous mulching has been going on for a long time—millions of years —by the time man first began to raise a few favored crops about 15,000 years ago.

Snow is not the only mulch that Nature has been using for all those centuries. We also know that leaves cover forest and woodland areas to protect the soil and feed its inhabitants. As the leaves fall to the forest floor, forming the basis of nature's mulch protection, they also decompose into a compost that makes up a rich soil-rebuilding program of nature. Out in the open fields, dead tops and foliage of the annual plants fall over to cover the ground and protect it from the rigors of winter.

This fact is important: composting and mulching go hand-in-hand and are, in many instances inseparable. Remember that in dealing with your soil. The aim is to build and maintain nature's complete soil pattern as far as possible. That demands a good organic mulch. The soil in your garden, whether you know it or not, is a world teaming with living things, whose combined activity enables the soil to grow plants.

In nature's scheme of things, as the dead remains of once living things gradually decompose, they return to the earth to be used again in a continuous cycle of life. Our soil will find itself undergoing conservation much more extensively and will be used more efficiently when we see Nature's pattern of natural mulching with its benefits according to the levels of soil fertility concerned. Mulching alone, as a mechanical ministration, cannot offset completely the shortage of fertility in the soil. Conversely, building up the fertility can be all the more reason for mulching also, a combination with doubled benefits because of the more efficient use of both the soil and the mulch that covers it. Of course, Mother Nature doesn't till or disturb her soil, except by using earthworms, insects and plant roots.

So, it's pretty apparent today that you're missing out on a lot of good gardening if you don't mulch—and mulch with whatever is cheap and handy. Leaves contain twice as much plant food as barnyard manure—pound for pound. Buckwheat hulls are fine, but so is hay. Sawdust will keep the weeds down and the soil moist, but be sure you add some form of nitrogen if you're going to raise a crop right away.

Our cumulative experience—and we already have well over a quarter of a century of it—and the experience of our readers has taught us to use whatever is cheap and abundant locally, to use it to get practical results and to solve our own gardening problems. We have learned to be our own "experts" and to think for ourselves.

And we've learned to mulch!

So, keep on mulching with whatever comes to hand —leaves, straw, hay, grass clippings, weeds, crop residues. Remember that the more humus you get into your soil, the better the crops you grow—while you're knocking the pesticides and herbicides out of your soil that somebody else put there.

Better break out the organic covering and start mulching—*now!*

Chapter One

MULCH–TOOL of the BEST DOGGONE ORGANIC GARDENERS

Constant correspondence with people who garden the organic way tells us they all agree that mulch is a must—and each for his own reasons. A Michigan gardener discovered it prevents weed takeovers. Another likes the hardiness it gives her plants against storms, while a desert-dweller lauds its ability to retain moisture for his garden.

Harold Fleck, the Michigan resident, found he could leave his garden unattended for periods of time during the summer without adverse effect. His mulch prevented weeds from crowding out his plants.

He was fortunate in that his garden area lay adjoining a field that was combined for clover seed the previous fall. After passing through the combine, the hay lay on the ground over winter. Fleck decided to use this handy supply of material for mulching. Early in the spring the

1

garden was plowed as usual. Then it was worked with a rotary tiller. As the various seeds were planted, the hay was placed between the rows of planted seeds. When the small seedlings came up, the hay was moved nearer to them. Finally, the whole garden was covered with hay.

"This new type of gardening has restored my once flagging interest in gardening," Fleck said, "The benefits were far more numerous than I had dreamed. The following are a few of the advantages I discovered:

"*Neatness.* It was always a problem to have a neat borderline between the grass of the lawn and the garden. Mulching solved this. Running the rotary mower right up to the mulch leaves no line of unmowed grass between the grass and the mulch. That narrow line of unmowed grass was always a problem before mulching.

"*No drought effects.* Although we had some very dry weather last summer our mulched garden did not show the effects of it. Our sweet corn did not 'roll' during the hottest days of the dry-weather period.

"*Pests subdued.* Before mulching, the beetles would ruin our lima and string beans. Last summer it was different. There were a few beetles, but they were too few to damage our production. No chemicals were used.

"It is wonderful to be able to walk out into the garden without getting dirt and dust in your shoes. The mulch is a soft and clean carpet to walk on. It is also a blessed relief to be free from the battle with weeds."

Fleck's experience also taught him that his mulch offered protection for his plants during bad weather and frost. When he feared an early frost was in the offing, he merely covered his plants with some straw in the evening, removing it in the morning. But Dorothy Schroeder's experience with mulch as a plant saver was more extensive. Hers involved a heavy storm.

"We should have known that it would happen after a completely rainless spring and early summer," she explained.

"Well, the day arrived when the rain came, a cloud-burst pouring down four inches of water in a little over an hour. It roared down the canyon east of the house in a white curtain, egged on by a 70-mile wind. During the worst of it, hail pelted the garden. Cracking branches of the old cottonwood trees were inaudible in the greater noise of the storm, so that we were surprised to find tree-sized limbs blocking both exits when the tempest stopped," she continued.

"After we had sawed a path through, we found what looked like complete devastation. The corn was flattened to the ground; the beautiful big crisp leaves of the summer squash and zucchini we'd been so proud of were broken and mud covered, soaked into the ground. The tomato supports had been broken or pulled out, and many tomato branches were broken off. Pepper plants were bent in the middle, their blooms stuck in the mud. The crisp green lettuce was reduced to mush.

"The first comfort I found in this devastation was that no water had run off my garden," Mrs. Schroeder said.

"Although our home is on a fairly steep hillside, the rain soaked into the mulch-covered soil while my neighbors's topsoil ran away in brown streams, clogging the drains and making extra work for the street department, and pointing out a valuable lesson. My neighbors complained that the rain was like the pounding of hammers on their soil; nothing soaked in and the ground was left like asphalt. My soil was cushioned by the mulch and there was no pounding.

"In general I learned from that storm that what seemed like complete devastation could be only a few days' setback if I moved in quickly", she continued. "I learned, too, that the plants growing in the best soil, richest in compost and most heavily covered with mulch, suffered least. That was brought home to me by the two potato patches. I planted one in the 'new' part of the garden, not yet prepared organically. For the other I used decayed leaf mold, planting the potatoes in a heap of it 18 inches above the level of the garden, between two thick layers. These potato plants weren't injured at all, but stood straight and tall after the storm. The others were beaten down to the ground," Mrs. Schroeder said.

"I also learned a lesson from a stone-mulched tomato. I had set the plant in a slight depression in the ground, and instead of staking it I had killed two birds with one stone by piling around it the rocks that I would have otherwise had to cart away, both to mulch it and to keep the branches off the ground. That was the first of the tomatoes to recover, with more of its leaves returning to their former healthy condition than I'd have thought possible. I was surprised, too, at how little the injured leaves affected the fruit bearing. Fruit bore better with their leaves whole, it's true, but production went on when they were ragged and full of holes," she explained.

Even more telling, Mrs. Schroeder said, was something that didn't immediately occur to her. "The roots weren't hurt at all. That, of course, accounted for the quick recovery of so many of our injured plants."

Ruth Tirell, a longtime organic gardener from Massachusetts, found through experience that a mulch works its wonders as well in the opposite extreme of weather—drought. Although the drought she experienced was unusually long and severe, no crop was a total loss. But the contrast between the plants that grew in bare, exposed soil and those that had been mulched was revealing. The favored crops which were mulched—tomatoes, summer squash, cucumbers and melons—all flourished and grew as if there were no drought.

The beans were another story. Compared to tomatoes, they have simple requirements—moderately good soil, some extra nourishment like compost in the furrow. She planted beans in late May. A little of the winter mulch was still visible; she didn't add to it—her beans had always done well enough.

June that year brought scant rain, only sprinkles. While, for various reasons, Mrs. Tirell didn't have much time for the garden, she did notice that the beans weren't growing fast. Still, she didn't water them. At maturity in July, the bean plants were stunted and the yield small, so she pulled them up. Usually her beans go into a second—and sometimes a third—blossoming and bearing.

Beets and carrots planted early in May were another example. Getting some quick growth before the drought started, they then seemed literally to stand still in the dry, baked, unmulched ground. All she got at harvest time were stunted, tough beets.

By contrast, the tomato patch was lush and green. Under the permanent mulch, the soil actually felt moist. The beans, the beets and carrots had all been planted in the same small garden, got the same treatment as the tomatoes—up to a point. All her crops, when planted, were given compost in the hole or furrow. But to nourish a plant, compost must be made soluble. During that long period when there were practically no rains, only the few crops she had kept mulched were really being fed.

In mid-July Mrs. Tirell made a test planting with summer squash, which she always starts at that time to take over in September when the early-planted crop is pulled up. She has found the new plants bear better fruit. She made two hills, treating both alike at first, digging in plenty of dried manure and compost, soaking the hills thoroughly on the day before and again on planting day.

Sowing the Seneca Buttercrunch hybrid, she left one hill bare but mulched the other with grass clippings. The next day she watered again, lifting the mulch on the second hill. She continued to water until the seeds sprouted at about the same time for both hills.

The mulched hill got no water from then on, except when she added to the mulch, while the bare-soil hill was watered every other day. Despite this neglect, the mulched plant grew faster during a period of practically no rain than the unmulched-but-watered-hill. It matured sooner, was bigger, leafier and more prolific—7 to

8 little squashes forming at one time and growing into healthy, big but tender, maturity. By contrast, the fruit from the unmulched hill were rather small and stringy.

At the height of the drought, about August 1, she made another test planting, this time with lettuce seedlings. While all were dressed with compost and the soil was soaked, half the seedlings were mulched and half were not.

When the unmulched lettuce was watered every day, the encrusted soil had to be broken with a hoe—which meant lots more work—so it would absorb the water. But the mulched lettuce was practically no trouble. Grass clippings were added once or twice, first soaking the old mulch which was dry on top but moist underneath. The unmulched lettuce succeeded—after all the care it had received—but the mulched plants succeeded even more, forming bigger, thicker, and more tender hearts to live up to Buttercrunch's reputation.

Like other organic gardeners, Ruth Tirell had known that mulches conserve moisture, but until that summer of abnormal drought, she hadn't seen with her own eyes the difference mulches do make at harvest time. From now on, she's joining other converts, like Arizona dweller Harold Rawson, and keeping her garden mulched year-round. Rawson joined the corps of converts when he found a combination of composting and mulching to be the best solution to the problem of gardening in a desert.

"Our mulch performs best when moist," Rawson said. "Evaporation cools the soil and plants just as our inexpensive evaporators cool many homes. But the mulch loses its moisture quickly in the desert sun, and this beneficial effect is lost. I've found that a screen wire held above smaller plants with a simple frame makes an excellent sun filter. The screen also offers considerable protection from the hot winds that blow in from the desert. Its only drawback is that it is not very attractive. Most of our garden takes a needed rest during the summer. Otherwise, we have no problems with our annual beds or the vegetable garden. During the enforced

A mulch of lawn clippings decomposes, converts to humus and enriches soil.

siesta, we thoroughly soak the soil to a depth of two or three feet, and then add compost, spading it in deeply and watering it. Anything that will add humus to the rather sparse earth is used—table scraps, composted crop residues and manure which we also use as a mulch. Thanks to our soil rebuilding program, the rows and beds are alive with earthworms most of the year," he added.

"With this preparation we have magnificent displays of flowers during March, April and May," Rawson continued, "And we do have delicious vegetables during the winter, plus some tomatoes and sweet corn in early summer.

"Growing roses and some shrubs creates perplexing problems here. Considerable composted material is used in the planting hole as a soil conditioner. Plants do very well for a couple years, then trouble starts. The acid reaction is lost as time passes, drainage may be impaired, and the leaves show salt damage. How do we restore healthy soil balance and functioning?

"We apply new mulch in liberal amounts, removing the old and spreading it around the garden," Rawson said. "Then we water deeply to wash the harmful salts down and out of the root zone. Since the bushes need more fertilizers to replace lost nutrients, I add manure and liquid fish solutions.

"When we came here five years ago, I was a bit confused by the problems confronting the desert gardener. While I may still be confused, one thing I'm firm about is this—mulching and composting combined is the surest way to gardening success in this hardpan country."

The grand old lady of mulching is without a doubt Ruth Stout. Ever since she moved to Redding, Connecticut back in 1929, Miss Stout has been dazzling her neighbors with her gardening technique. It's a unique one, because it succeeds despite the fact that she doesn't plow, harrow, spade, hoe, weed or cultivate.

Just what is this gal's secret? Very briefly, it's an over-all year-round mulch, and a thick one at that. Six to eight inches of hay, weeds, paper and garden wastes placed around every flower and vegetable, shrub and tree. It is never turned under, never disturbed; it is, in effect, a constantly decomposing compost pile spread over all the places where rich earth should abound.

"Right under the mulch you'll find earthworms crawling around in the moist earth in the driest weather," she said. "It defeats the drought; it does away with all the heavy work of gardening. And it can improve your garden's appearance.

"Now let's say you want to start a garden in a spot which is now sod, or full of perennial weeds," she explained. "If you mulch it heavily in early fall it will be rotted sufficiently by spring so that you can put in a garden without bothering to plow. It's possible that for small seeds you may have to do a bit of sod-shaking but nothing like what has to be done if one plows sod in spring and then tries to plant.

"For tomatoes, or any other crop which calls for putting in plants instead of seeds, nothing could be simpler," she said. "Pull back the mulch a bit and stick the plant in the ground. And for things grown from seed but which should be thinned to 12 or 18 inches apart, such as the cabbage family—well, you can plant these in hills, a few seeds in each spot, thinning them later to one plant.

"Onion sets may just be scattered around on last year's mulch, then covered with a few inches of loose hay; by this method you can 'plant' a pound of them in a few minutes, and you may do it, if you like, before the ground thaws. Lettuce seeds, too, will germinate if merely thrown on frozen earth—but not on top of mulch. And this, of course, can't be done if you plow before planting.

"Many people," Miss Stout said, "have discovered that they can lay seed potatoes on last year's mulch, or on the ground or even on sod, cover them with about a foot of loose hay, and later simply pull back the mulch and pick up the new potatoes.

"A few weeds may come through your mulch here and there; this will be because you didn't apply it thickly enough to defeat them. They are easy to pull if you want to take the trouble, but the simplest thing is to just toss a bit of hay on top of them," she said. "And if a row of something needs thinning, this can be done effectively by simply covering the plants you want to get rid of with a little mulch."

There are other benefits, too. She hasn't sprayed her garden for years but hasn't had pest problems. The crows, she said, are nonplussed by the heavy layer of mulch over her corn. And she hasn't used fertilizer for years, either. "After you have mulched for a year to two," she said, "you will need no fertilizer of any kind except perhaps for a little meal (cottonseed, soybean— whatever you can buy) for nitrogen. The rotting mulch supplies all the nourishment your plants should have.

"A word of caution: after your soil has become so nearly perfect because of so much rotting mulch in it, you may be swamped with the quantity of your crops."

It was just this sort of Ruth Stout warning that got Dorothy Anderson, a Wisconsinite, moving. She decided that if Ruth Stout could garden from her couch, so could she. At any rate, she had nothing to lose by giving it a try.

"In our garden, head lettuce was tennis-ball size; cucumbers, exhausted fending off the cucumber beetles, stretched only to fountain-pen length. And strawberries —well, it might take 50 to fill one English teacup," Mrs. Anderson explained. But after she and her family started mulching, it seemed that she was merely replacing one evil with another.

"Pleasure driving through the country ceased to exist," she explained. "My eye spied any spoiled hay within a block of the highway. After hectic dickering with the owner, we loaded the car with mulch. It's heavy, dirty and scratchy—but what does that matter compared to salvaging two whole bales of spoiled hay?

"The first two bales spread in the middle of the garden looked as lonesome as a fly in the middle of a duck pond. When we tried to cover our 30-by-80 foot garden with mulch, it suddenly expanded to city-park size.

"Mulching took on the attributes of a nightmare. The garden opened its jaws and gulped down mulch far faster than we could provide it. When we walked down the rows of mulch it snapped, crackled and shrank. When it rained, the mulch became soft and gushy and shrank. When the sun dried it, it shriveled and shrank. Under the winter snow it all but disappeared," she said.

"In the spring the need for more mulch to cover the garden's nakedness was renewed. The old nightmare chugged and chased our heels. If Ruth Stout could do it, why couldn't we? We hauled in sawdust, spoiled hay, more sawdust, marshgrass, wood chips, spoiled hay. We salvaged the cut grass along the roadside. Every leaf that blew in the wind was gathered and added to the mulch. Every blade of grass, every weed, was pounced on for mulch.

"After 5 years of constant mulching my temperature has subsided to normal. I, too, lie on my couch by the window and anticipate the first head of lettuce sprouting a blue ribbon from its leaves, and I picture a new garden cart sturdy enough to haul to the house the 30-pound Blue Hubbard squash," she continued.

"My anticipation of a beautiful garden has truly been realized. The giant heads of Boston lettuce actually did bring in a blue ribbon. With the drought we've had in Wisconsin for the last 7 summers, this would have been impossible without mulching."

Dorothy spoke for all mulchers when she concluded, "The proof of its value is under the mulch. The earth is soft, moist and full of earthworms (just as Ruth Stout said). I have longed for a garden soil so soft that I could scoop out a trench for seeds with my hands.

"My dream has come true; *the mulch made it possible.*"

Chapter Two

MULCH
and YOUR SOIL

Mulching will improve any type of soil, generally speaking. But before using fertilizers you should know something about the make-up of *your* soil.

What kind of soil do you have? That's an easy question to ask, a difficult one to answer. Replies could vary from "hard as a rock" or "a sandy loam with a pH of 6.5" to "a deep soil of podzolic origin."

To some people, soil is nothing more than dirt that's perfectly okay as long as it allows flowers and most of the lawn to grow, and when muddy, doesn't get the house or patio too messed up.

Fortunately, to the majority of us, our soil represents a great deal more than that. Unscientific as it may be, we still regard soil as a living, breathing organism with definite likes and dislikes. It has a personality all its own

14

—depending upon its past history, treatment and present environment.

In the *Yearbook of Agriculture,* published by the U.S. Department of Agriculture, Roy Simonson writes:

"Soil is related to the earth much as the rind is related to an orange. But this rind of the earth is far less uniform than the rind of an orange. It is deep in some places and shallow in others. It may be red, as soils are in Hawaii, or it may be black, as they are in North Dakota.

"Be it deep or shallow, red or black, sand or clay, the soil is the link between the rock core of the earth and the living things on its surface. It is the foothold for the plants we grow. Therein lies the main reason for our interest in soil.

"Every soil consists of mineral and organic matter, water and air. The proportions vary, but the major components remain the same."

All soils have a profile—a succession of layers in a vertical section down into loose, weathered rock. The individual layers are called horizons. The upper layers of the soil profile, known as the "A" horizon, generally contain the most organic matter, bacteria and fungi, and are darkened as a result. This upper layer is the surface soil with which we are most familiar.

The subsoil, or "B" horizon, lies directly below, and is also markedly weathered but usually contains little or no organic matter. In temperate-region soils, the subsoil layers average between three and four feet deep.

The layers where the subsoil merges into the original soil material is known as the "C" horizon. It's usually weathered, and the upper portion is about to become a part of the lower subsoil.

Soil is a natural body; its formation depends mostly on climate, living organisms, parent rocks, topography and time. Because of the variations in these five factors, soils in any one region are far from identical.

Although soil composition is complex, regard it— and the entire process of soil formation—as a marvelous work of nature rather than saying: "It's a mystery to

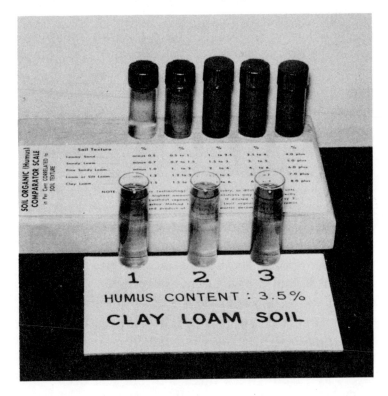

Soil type must be determined according to information provided in kits before the test for humus content is made.

me, so let's get on with the actual gardening work." Once we have the attitude that we *can* learn more about our soils, we'll be going a long way to finding out its needs, and what should be done to improve it.

Your home grounds probably consist of a lawn, shrubs, trees, flowers and vegetables—all supported by the soil beneath them. The goal is to learn what general type of soil you have, if it has enough of the major nutrient elements and whether it's acid or alkaline. The answers to these questions will tell you how to plant an effective soil build-up program and what plants will grow best in it.

There are two ways to find out the nutritional deficiencies of the soil. A soil sample may be sent to a commercial laboratory or to a state agricultural experiment station. Or a home testing kit may be acquired and the necessary tests made on the spot.

A home test kit is particularly valuable since it makes periodic testing of the soil practical. Indeed, the more it is used, the less costly it becomes on a per-test cost basis. Most of the kits are simple to use and require no knowledge of chemistry or laboratory procedure. And they'll quickly reveal the deficiencies of the soil.

All soils are composed of particles varying greatly in size and shape. In order to classify them by texture as well as physical properties, four fundamental soil groups are recognized: gravels, sands, loams and clays. (The last three make up most of the world's arable lands.)

The sand group includes all soils of which the silt and clay make up less than 20 percent by weight. Its mineral particles are visible to the naked eye and are irregular in shape. Because of this, their water-holding capacity is low, but they possess good drainage and aeration and are usually in a loose, friable condition.

In contrast, particles in a clay soil are very fine (invisible under ordinary microscope) and become sticky and cement-like.

Texture of the loam class cannot be as clearly defined, since its mechanical composition is about midway between sand and clay. Professors T. Lyon and Harry Buckman in their excellent book, *The Nature and Properties of Soils,* describe loams "as such a mixture of sand, silt and clay particles as to exhibit light and heavy properties in about equal proportions . . . Because of this intermixture of coarse, medium and fine particles, usually they possess the desirable qualities both of sand and clay without exhibiting those undesirable properties, as extreme looseness and low water capacity on the one hand and stickiness, compactness, and very slow air and water movement on the other."

Fortunately for the gardeners and farmers in the United States, most soils are in the loam classification. The majority of soils are mixtures; the more common class names appear below: (Combinations are given when one size of particles is evident enough to affect the texture of the loam. For example, a loam in which sand is dominant will be classified as a sandy loam of some kind.)

Sandy Soils

Gravelly sands
Coarse sands

Medium sands
Fine sands
Loamy sands

Loamy Soils

Coarse sandy loams
Medium sandy loams
Fine sandy loams
Silty loams and stony silt loams
Clay loams

Clayey Soils

Stony clays
Gravelly clays
Sandy clays
Silty clays
Clays

You can get a good idea of your soil's texture and class by merely rubbing it between the thumb and the fingers or in the palm of the hand. Sand particles are gritty; silt has a floury or talcum-powder feel when dry, and is only moderately plastic when moist, while the clayey material is harsh when dry and very plastic and sticky when wet.

Professors Lyon and Buckman observe: "This method is used in all field operations, especially in soil survey, land classification and the like. Accuracy . . . can be acquired by the careful study of known samples." If you're interested in developing an ability to classify soils, we suggest your contacting the local county agent for soil samples that are correctly classified.

While on the subject of soil characteristics, let's take a look at how the structure of your soil influences gardening results. Structure refers to the arrangements or groupings of the soil particles. The two extremes are "single-grained", as loose sand, and "massive", where the soil masses are very large, irregular and featureless.

The ideal structure is granular, where the rounded aggregates (or clusters) of soil lie loosely and readily shake apart. When the granules are especially porous, the term crumb is applied.

How can you change your soil's structure to a granular condition? The answer is clearly given by Lyon and Buckman:

"The major agency in the encouragement of granulation probably is organic matter, especially as it undergoes decay and is synthesized into humus. Not only does it bind but it lightens and expands, making possible the tremendous porosity so characteristic of individual soil crumbs. Plant roots probably promote granulation as much or more by the decay of the distributed organic matter as by the disruptive actions of the root material. The electrochemical properties of humus, no doubt, are fully effective in the organization and the later stabilization of the aggregates.

". . . At the same time organic matter promotes ready air and water movement and, not only does it lower the plasticity and cohesion of the soil mass, but it also localizes the influence of clay, since this constituent seems to be concentrated in the newly formed aggregates. . . . In fact, the granulation of a clay soil cannot be promoted adequately without the presence of a certain amount of humus. The maintenance of organic matter, therefore, is of great practical concern . . ."

Of course, the two soil experts were speaking chiefly in terms of the physical characteristics of soil. But maintenance of organic matter in soil is beneficial chemically and biologically as well as physically. Soil scientists working for the U.S. Department of Agriculture have tested the effects of organic matter in soil. They tried it on rotation. They tried it on tillage. They tried it on fertility. In every case, they found that organic matter improves the soil and helps plants to grow fat and nutritious.

A number of interesting concepts on the value of organic matter in soil were suggested to the Nebraska Crop Improvement Association by T. M. McCalla, a bacteriologist with the agriculture department's Soil Conservation Service in Lincoln, Nebraska.

McCalla said that organic matter is indispensable to plant growth. However, he said most of our food is produced by plants grown on soils with organic matter in them. And soils with more organic matter in them produce higher yields than soils with less organic matter.

This is about the same as saying that humans don't have to have solid food to live on. We don't! But who wants to live on soup and milk for the rest of their lives, when such things as steak, mashed potatoes, gravy, and fresh fruit are available? And don't you feel like you can do a better day's work when you have a good meal in your stomach? The same way with plants. They have been found to do better when raised on soils with plenty of organic matter present. Even such plants as tomatoes and gardenias which have been raised on nutrient solutions have been found to do better on a good soil.

Organic matter benefits the soil in numerous ways, McCalla pointed out, through its biological, chemical, and physical effects. One important benefit, he said, comes from its influence on the activities of soil microorganisms which release plant nutrients. Other benefits come from soil nitrogen tied up in organic matter, and the ability of organic matter to stabilize soil structure, increase aggregation, aeration, water-holding capacity, and decrease soil erosion and runoff. All of these increase crop yields.

Soil organic matter, he said, is that part of the soil which originates from plants, animals and microbes. Humus is the dark organic matter of the soil that has undergone decomposition until it can no longer be recognized as the original organic material. Mix any plant residue with soil and it becomes a part of the soil organic matter. When it decomposes it becomes humus.

This is the miracle substance that makes life possible. Without it there would be little or no plant life on earth. Proper use of humus can make soil more fertile, yields more abundant, and foods more nutritious.

One way humus builds up soil and brings abundant yields of healthy, nourishing vegetables and fruits to your dinner table is by making minerals available. Humus does this primarily by chelation, solvation, and storage.

Chelation is the word scientists use to describe the claw-like action of the organic compounds in humus. Some of these compounds stretch out like an earthworm. As they swim around in the soil water they come into contact with minerals in rocks. When they do, both ends swing close together and grab hold of the mineral. The claw that is formed is so strong that it can yank an atom of mineral right out of a piece of rock. This gets the mineral out in the open where plants can use it for food. Soil scientists in the University of Illinois' agronomy department have explained that "the availability of plant nutrients may be greatly affected by the chelating ability of organic matter."

They also explained another trick humus has for making soil minerals available to plants. It is called solvation. "During the decomposition of plant residues," the scientists explained, "certain acids, particularly carbonic acid, are formed that dissolve soil minerals and make the nutrients more available to the plant."

One of the most important properties of humus is its ability to store mineral nutrients. Department of Agriculture soil scientists have said that "humus is like a sponge in absorbing water and helps hold mineral elements in the upper soil layers. It is the seat of the greatest microbiological activity and acts as a nutrient reservoir." Agricultural experiments have shown that humus supplies plants with 95 per cent of the nitrogen they need, up to 60 per cent of the phosphorus, up to 80 per cent of the sulphur and similar amounts of other minerals. These minerals are supplied to the plant as the plant needs them for food.

But is it organic matter in itself or its decay that is important to soils?

As soon as organic matter is incorporated with soil

or applied to the surface of it, it is immediately attacked by a host of microbes of every kind and description. These are the microorganisms that cause the organic matter to decay and be dissipated in a short time under normal garden or field conditions. These microorganisms are so active that any average soil is able to handle easily many times the amount of organic matter usually applied to it.

A "packed", mud-pie soil can be made workable with mulch.

Since the microorganisms readily attack the organic matter and soon convert it into humus and other decay products, the question comes up of whether it is desirable to have at least some undecomposed organic matter in the soil. "Yes," is the answer to that. The undecomposed organic matter continues to furnish food for the microorganisms. It also acts as a rough conditioner to open up and aerate the soil. It allows rain to

Soil mulched consistently is well aerated, easily worked and full of nutrients.

25

soak down into the soil and helps to prevent wind and rain erosion. Hence, it is necessary to keep applying organic matter to soils, regardless of whether they are garden or farmland. And regardless of whether the organic matter is available or not, it is still needed by soil microorganisms.

But what about the benefits other than from the rough organic matter? There is no question about benefits. The principal benefit is the release of plant nutrients caused by the microbial action and the chelating action of the organic matter. Of particular importance are the nitrogen and phosphorous released during the decomposition of the organic matter. These help dissolve minerals in the soil such as phosphorous, potash, calcium, magnesium and other essential plant nutrients. Chelation occurring when decomposing organic matter comes into contact with the minerals in the soil make iron, copper and other metals available to plants.

Since microorganisms are most active during the period of plant growth due to warmer temperatures, essential plant nutrients are also made most available during this period. In other words, the dynamic life of the soil is most active when it is most needed.

Another little considered effect of the decomposition of organic materials in soil is the production of "auximones" and other growth-promoting substances. There is also the production of toxic or antibiotic substances when green manures are added to the soil. Strangely enough, these toxic substances do not harm the growing plants. They appear to help in controlling root-rot and damping-off fungi.

The benefits from organic matter, then, are due

primarily to the activity of the microorganisms which decompose the organic matter and to the products they form. But the organic matter is also important to the chemical composition of the soil.

"Soil organic matter contains the things that plants have taken from the soil, air and water, as well as products resulting from the decomposition of plants and animal materials by soil microorganisms," McCalla noted in his report. "It contains generally about 56 per cent carbon, 5 per cent nitrogen, and oxygen, hydrogen, phosphorus, sulphur, calcium, magnesium, potassium, iron, zinc, manganese, copper and boron. Organic matter also contains numerous organic compounds. A ton of wheat straw will produce about one and one-half tons of carbon dioxide. Decomposition of soil organic matter results in the gradual production of mineral elements in forms that are available to plants. A storehouse of plant nutrients, organic matter is almost a fool-proof fertilizer.

How much organic matter do good farm soils contain? The better farm soils, McCalla said, contain from four to five per cent organic matter. How to maintain this is the big problem. Continuous cropping to cultivated plants reduces the organic matter content of the soil. However, organic matter was maintained at about the same level or higher in experiments by the liberal use of manure, sod crops, and wise crop rotations, McCalla said.

Soil scientists recommend adding a generous supply of organic matter to soil at frequent intervals. This keeps biodynamic activity at its peak. Compost may be added any time. Undecomposed materials such as grass clippings, leaves, shredded corn stalks, alfalfa, clover and so on are best turned under after the fall harvest. If you do three things—give plants plenty of sunshine, plenty of water and add generous amounts of compost —you will be sure of supplying the basic nutritional requirements of plants. The net result will be a better soil more capable of growing larger crops of more nutritious fruits and vegetables.

But how does mulch fit into the picture?

Well, most obviously, it is a constant supply of organic matter for the soil. As it decomposes, it provides the important microbiological activity. And as it decomposes, it becomes humus.

An important benefit of mulch is its improvement of soil structure and tilth. As the decaying organic matter works down into the soil, it becomes more friable, is better penetrated by water and its aeration is improved, thus stimulating root and biological activity. If organic mulch is mixed into the upper soil layer, it will dilute the soil and usually increase root growth. When mulches such as crushed corn cobs, sphagnum peat moss, or sawdust are used, the effect of the addition of this material to the soil is almost immediate. On clay soils, aeration is increased. Water holding capacity is increased in a sandy soil, an important function of mulch which is often overlooked. A mulch of leaves, grass or dead plant residues cuts down evaporation, helps to hold moisture in the soil and lowers the soil temperature. Sandy soils mulched with grass and leaves in November have shown 2 to 3 per cent more moisture the following May than unmulched soil. While this is a small amount, it is sufficient to make the difference between good plant growth and little or no growth.

Plant roots extend down into the soil in search of moisture. In so doing, ordinarily, they grow away from the highest concentration of the mineral plant food elements. With a good mulch of organic matter the surface soil is kept moist, promoting the development of feeder roots near the surface of the soil, the zone of highest fertility. The improved moisture condition and increased plant food constituents result in increased vigor and better plant growth. A mulch will prove beneficial on heavy textured soils as well as on light textured ones, but the benefit from improved moisture conditions will be greatest on sandy soils.

Mulches improve and stabilize soil structure or the arrangement of soil articles. Because of the mulch layer, the soil structure is not disturbed by pelting rain, or coarse streams or drops of water from irrigation devices. Some gardeners do not realize that cultivation of the soil when it is too wet destroys good soil structure. When mulches are used, the danger of cultivation at the wrong time is eliminated since very little, if any, cultivation is necessary. Another way to harm the soil structure is walking on the soil when it is wet. If there is a mulch on the soil, this will serve as a cushion and the compaction of the soil is reduced.

If the mulch is not well-decomposed but is a decomposable material, it will promote granulation of soil particles just as Lyon and Buckman said. During decomposition of the organic material, soil microorganisms secrete a sticky material which promotes the granulation of the soil. This is especially true of heavy soil types. Materials like sphagnum peat moss, which decompose slowly, have little effect on granulation. Straw, hay, fresh leaves, or manure, which decompose rather rapidly, do have an effect on granulation.

A valuable organic matter is formed during the decomposition or rotting of a mulch cover. Decomposition is not an undesirable process, but rather one that recirculates necessary plant food elements for additional crops. In addition to the release of mineral elements such as nitrogen, phosphorus, iron, carbon dioxide and water are released.

All mulch covers do not decompose at the same rate. More resistant substances in the mulch cover, such as lignin, undergo relatively slow change because of their complex nature. Lignin, together with cellulose, forms the chief part of woody tissue. Carbohydrates, such as plant sugars and cellulose, on the other hand, are rapidly attacked yielding carbon dioxide and water. The resistant materials like lignin are not wholly inert nor are they readily identified in the soil. If this were not so, organic mulch would accumulate until ultimately the surface of the earth would be covered by it.

When an organic mulch decomposes, it is similar to a wood fire which dies down from a bright blaze to smoldering embers, glowing for a long time.

The composition of organic matter from different locations is surprisingly uniform despite the wide variations in type of plants and microorganisms that are responsible for its formation. Recent investigations indicate that three classes of compounds dominate soil organic matter. They are substances produced by the alteration of lignin of plants, compounds related to carbohydrates (bacterial gums, slimes and molds) and material probably derived from proteins. The last is probably the principal carrier of nitrogen.

The lignin of the organic mulch undergoes change when first mixed in the soil. After the initial attack a resistant portion remains that is so greatly altered as not to be properly spoken of as lignin. This portion is usually resistant to further degradation.

The carbohydrate-like materials in an organic mulch are largely substances of microbial origin, as, slimes, gums and organic salts of uronic, teichoic, muramie fulvic and humic acids.

There are, of course, many other benefits derived from mulching. Not all are as complex as those involving chelation and solvation and other processes in the soil. But they are vital to growth of nutritious fruits and vegetables. They are vital to the maintenance of a good, fertile soil. They can be stated briefly.

—Mulching conserves soil moisture by reducing the evaporation of water from the soil.

—Mulching prevents crusting of the soil surface, thus improving absorption and percolation of water to the soil areas where the roots are growing.

—Mulching maintains a more uniform soil temperature by acting as an insulator that keeps the soil warm during cool spells and cooler during the warm months of the year.

—Mulching reduces weed problems when the mulch material itself is weed-free and is applied thickly enough to prevent weed seed germination or smother existing smaller weeds. Mulching thus considerably reduces the time and labor expended in weeding garden areas.

—Mulching adds to the beauty of the landscape by

providing a cover of uniform color which can be neutral or non-detracting and may add an interesting texture to an otherwise drab surface.

—Mulching can prevent fruit and plants from becoming mud-splashed and reduce losses to soil-borne diseases.

—Mulching can prevent freezing injuries caused by late spring or early fall frosts if a light layer of mulch material is placed on top of the plants in the evening and removed in the morning.

It is important to remember that mulching should be done only with natural, organic materials. And for good reason. The soil, basically, is made up of weathered rock particles and organic matter, closely associated and intermixed.

In the organic method of gardening, we attempt to feed the soil so its natural constitution is not disturbed, basing our procedures and techniques on the study of the makeup of the soil. Knowing how it was originally formed, we can better understand what kind of food will suit it.

The soil's basic elements—inorganic minerals from rock fragments, organic matter, water and air—logically lead us to the best formula for its sustenance. If we restore the used-up mineral and organic matter, and if we see to it that there is an adequacy of water and air, the fertility of the soil will continue to maintain itself. The great forests, the huge groves of trees and masses of vegetation which we know exist unaided by man, are all growing within the scope of this simple formula— straight, unadulterated mineral matter, organic matter, water and air. The great redwood trees of the western coast which tower into the clouds depend on nothing more than these four things.

Therefore, when we mulch the earth with only the elements of which it is naturally constituted, we are not gambling. And since the gardener will soon discover that he can secure a greater harvest of vegetables by following the organic system, he will realize how wrong the chemical method is.

Chapter Three

MULCH and YOUR GARDEN

Mulching will do as much for your garden as it will for your soil, for there are as many benefits of mulching above-ground as there are in-ground.

While the mulch is stimulating and feeding aeration, microbiological activity and granulation in your soil, it will be preserving moisture and soil structure, maintaining a fairly constant temperature, quelling weeds, disease and insects, making your garden something worth looking at and its produce worth eating.

Mrs. Robert Smith of Fort Wayne, Indiana, praises the mulch system. She and her husband, both practitioners of the organic way of gardening, tried the mulch system for the first time several years ago when they were planning a four-week vacation far from the vegetable patch. Mrs. Smith planted the garden to coincide with their return and thoroughly mulched about three-quarters of the plot.

"My husband was rather disgruntled that I spent money for the mulch," she said, "but on our return he had to admit I had been wise. Needless to say, the area I did not mulch was stunted in growth although there was a great harvest of weeds. The rest of the garden was a veritable jungle of beans, corn, cucumbers, and a dozen other vegetables, with few weeds showing. Our yields were fantastic—the best year we'd ever had in growing a garden!" she continued.

"Later, in talking to my neighbors, they said not one drop of rain had fallen during our month's absence, and they couldn't understand why my garden had survived and was so luxurious and rich in color as well as crops while their gardens either dried up or were badly stunted.

"This year we plan to be gone again for 4 to 5 weeks, so we'll again be mulching heavily and expect a bumper crop waiting our return. It's really been a pleasure gardening organically and seeing our production outdo itself each year," she concluded.

Mrs. Smith's testimonial is typical for the mulch-it-and-virtually-forget-it way of gardening. Ruth Stout has been practicing it for years. And mulching has been around for many more years than Ruth Stout—and that's a lot of years.

The fact that the effects of mulching are seldom simple complicates the search for precise information. Certain patterns of behavior of soils and plants under mulch, however, have been observed in studies conducted in the United States and abroad. These studies have determined the effects of mulch on the soil, as outlined in the previous chapter. They have determined that mulching affects such gardening conditions as moisture, soil structure, temperature, weed growth, plant disease and insect infestation. Further, mulch can be a factor in the appearance of a garden, although appearance isn't the sort of thing you pin down with a scientific test or study.

Temperature and moisture or a combination of the two frequently appear to be the most critical factors in determining the effect of mulch on crop yield. For Mrs. Smith, for example, the moisture holding qualities of a good mulch were critical not just to a good yield, but to the simple survival of her garden.

Farmers who use mulches generally do because it is the best way to make most efficient use of the available moisture in producing crops. In most cases, the moisture content of the surface soil under mulch is higher than when soil is clean-cultivated.

But where does this moisture come from if—as in Mrs. Smith's case—there is no rainfall for a substantial period of time? The moisture comes from the dew. Dew is the condensation of moisture from the air in the soil. Most of the dew is a complete waste as far as plant growth is concerned—unless there is something on the surface to catch it and prevent it from evaporating. A mulch is a wonderful dew-catcher. A mulch of rocks or wooden boards catches more dew than any other because no air or moisture can pass through it.

While much of the Northeast was enduring its fourth consecutive summer of searing drought several seasons ago, and worried communities began placing more restrictions on water use, the helpful role that a mulch can play became increasingly apparent. A notable instance was the attractive Brooklyn Botanical Gardens, where regular irrigation was curtailed completely in the midst of New York's drive to conserve water. Instead, mulching was employed around the many gardens and plantings. The dampness underneath could be felt as well as seen and an increase of earthworms resulted in the soil where areas were mulched.

Experiments in a number of states have shown the efficiency of mulch in holding down evaporation. The amount of moisture savings attributable to reduced evaporation under a straw mulch varied widely with climate and other varying test conditions. In experiments in Tennessee and Michigan, for example, indirect measurements showed that, in humid areas, evaporation losses may be reduced by the use of mulch. The reductions ranged from around 12 or 16 per cent to as much as 50 per cent or more.

Other experiments in North Carolina showed that wheat straw mulch at three tons per acre increased moisture in the soil and markedly increased corn yields during drought conditions. The increases averaged 21 bushels per acre in eight experiments, with a close ratio between corn yields and moisture content of the soil. In 10 experiments conducted under good moisture conditions, mulching did not greatly affect yields.

Similarly with tobacco, there is a close correlation between drought conditions and the effect of mulching on crop yields. Agricultural researchers working in Maryland found that tobacco grown under four to six tons of straw mulch per acre gave yields as good as those from cultivated fields during five years when rain was normal or less than normal—but crop values were reduced during two years of above normal rainfall.

On land where excess moisture is a problem because of poor drainage and heavy rainfall, mulching could obviously have an adverse effect.

The second most critical factor appears to be temperature. A mulched plant is not subjected to the extremes of temperature that an exposed plant is. Unmulched roots are damaged by the heaving of soil brought on by sudden thaws and frosts. The mulch acts as an insulating blanket, keeping the soil warmer in winter and cooler in summer.

Soil heaving damage, brought on by a winter of sudden, deep freezes alternated with abrupt thaws, should be no threat. Safe under a protective mulch, plants and topsoil can wait out the severest winter weather with an absolute minimum of injury.

The penalty for not mulching can be high at any time. But the advent of winter can bring real trouble to the thinly mulched or unmulched flower beds and vegetable patch. Winter-hardy perennials can be lifted literally out of the ground by frost action and their roots exposed. Wheat plants are frequently completely heaved out of the soil, taprooted legumes such as alfalfa can be badly injured, while entire fall-planted beds of strawberries may be found dead or dying above the ground.

It generally is not known that the type of soil has more to do with soil heaving than the prevailing climate. Sandy soils rarely heave because they are well-drained and the free water is below the three-foot mark —which is as deep as the soil freezes. Soil heaving is not caused by the expansion of water freezing in the soil but by the formation of more ice from water moving up through the soil.

Heaving occurs when the surface layer of the soil freezes and is pushed upward by pure ice columns of "lenses" which develop just below the layer of frozen earth. The pillars of ice are formed by water that swells upward from below to the lower side of the frozen layer, moving by capillary action through pores or voids in the soil structure.

Control of heaving may not be possible under really severe circumstances, but the place of mulching in maintaining control is nevertheless secure. Good drainage reduces the chances of heaving injury by removing free water near the surface. A good blanket of mulch further reduces the possibility of heaving by controlling the action of the water in the soil—preventing it from alternately freezing and thawing and freezing again.

A good mulch has a similarly tempering effect on the soil's reaction to the change of seasons. It soothes the swing into spring and blunts the first bitter blows of fall and winter weather.

In experiments using mulches on vegetables, researchers of the Pennsylvania State Agricultural Experiment Station concluded that reduced temperatures under mulches in the early spring might partly explain smaller early yields and greater total yields in midsummer when lower soil temperatures would have a favorable result. The mulch tempers day-to-day temperature changes and even the rise and fall of the temperature in the course of the day.

There are a number of factors which enter into the

mulch's ability to temper temperature, one of which is the color of the mulch material. Light-colored materials tend to reflect heat rays while dark-colored mulches tend to absorb them.

This was brought out in a Kansas study which showed that the darkening of a straw mulch by humification influenced the effect the mulch had on the soil's summer temperature. Under a light-colored, fresh mulch the soil temperature was 2.8° C. lower than in bare soil, while soil under a dark gray, partially decomposed mulch was only 0.2° C. lower than bare soil. Reflection from the fresh, light-colored mulch was about three times as great as from the dark, partially decomposed mulch: 32 candles of light per square foot as compared to 11 candles.

To a degree, the moisture preserving and temperature controlling characteristics of mulches are tied to their ability to maintain good soil structure. A mulch prevents—largely by preserving the moisture in the ground —crusting of the earth. A crusted earth is more subject to erosion by wind and rain and is less capable of absorbing the moisture of a brief shower. Indeed, such showers even contribute to the crusting of the earth by compacting it.

Mulches protect the soil from the direct impact of rainfall. Raindrops fall with tremendous force. When this force strikes on bare ground, much of the energy is expended by breaking up soil aggregates and sealing and compacting the surface soil. This decreases the infiltration capacity of the soil and increases runoff and erosion. By breaking the force and size of the falling raindrops, surface mulches maintain soil porosity and conserve soil and water.

The preservation of porosity was demonstrated in U. S. Department of Agriculture tests in Ohio. The results of the tests indicated that the greater penetration of water generally occurring in mulched soils was primarily due to the protection that the cover affords to an existing favorable soil structure. But when the soil wasn't permeable to begin with, putting mulch on the surface did not cause the water to penetrate. After cultivating the soil to a one-inch depth to break surface crust, however, the infiltration rate under mulching after 60 minutes was 2.10 inches an hour as compared to 0.28 inches an hour on similar unmulched plots.

Similarly, the value of mulches in controlling erosion is widely recognized and has been test proven. Mulches do this by reducing runoff, by maintaining the porosity of the soil and by providing conditions favorable to the activity of organisms which can result in more stable soil aggregates. These all interrelate and all contribute to the soil-saving effect of the mulch.

The extent of this effect has been measured in numerous studies. In Illinois tests, for example, soil losses after an hour's rain of 1-3/4 inches were 3,225 pounds per acre from bare ground as compared to 205 pounds from ground mulched with cornstalks.

In studies recently conducted in cooperation with the Georgia Agricultural Experiment Station, researchers found that a mulch of pine needles, straw, or any other cheap mulching material applied at the rate of around two tons per acre could be used successfully to prevent erosion on steep road banks until a cover of vegetation could be established. The chief landscape architect for the Ohio Department of Highways has said that mulch is a primary part of his state's successful seeding operation. He said that straw mulch was first used on highway seeding to protect sloping areas from erosion. Its use has been continued because the straw successfully extended the seeding season. As a result, seeding is done at any time of the year that a proper seed bed can be secured. Usually a thicker amount of straw is required if the project is to go through a dormant seeding period, he noted.

Soybeans on the right, grown with an oat straw mulch, are almost weed-free, in marked contrast to unmulched beans at left.

Public Works magazine observed that "the best thinking has found that mulch is of great benefit because it reduces erosion; it reduces the force of raindrops; it reduces evaporation; it keeps the seed bed loose and at a more even soil temperature; and it eventually adds organic matter to the soil. Mulch shades the seedlings, allowing some sunlight to penetrate and air to circulate, and it encourages and hastens native growth in areas that have not been seeded."

But there's even more of a case for mulching than that, because mulching protects plants from weeds, insects and soil-borne diseases.

Ruth Stout is most outspoken on the value of mulches for weed-control. In her recent book *The Ruth Stout No-Work Garden Book,* she explained why mulches are good for controlling weed growth.

"If the mulch is thick enough, the weeds can't come through," she wrote. "When I say this, people then invariably ask why it is that the vegetable seeds come through and weed seeds don't; this is because heavy mulch is on top of the latter, but not the former . . .

"A few weeds may come through your mulch here and there; this will be because you didn't apply it thickly enough to defeat them," she continued. "They are easy to pull if you want to take the trouble, but the simplest thing is to just toss a bit of hay on top of them."

A good mulch will also deter garden pests. Ruth Stout has reported that corn-hungry crows are "nonplussed" by her mulch. She and other mulchers, like Harold Fleck, have lauded the freedom from insects that a thick mulch brings. "Before mulching", Fleck said, "the beetles would ruin our lima and string beans.

Last summer it was different." He had mulched for the first time. "There were a few beetles, but they were too few to damage our production."

Or as Ruth Stout puts it, "I haven't sprayed for 18 years and have no bug problems at all except for a few Japanese beetles which go for soybeans and raspberries. No bean beetles, no aphis, not a potato bug, no corn worms."

Plants, fruits and vegetables are also protected from soil-borne diseases. Mud is less of a problem when walking on mulched rows. Low-growing plants aren't splashed with mud. Free from this, they are also apt to be free from diseases that mud splashed on them might carry.

At harvest time, vegetables which sprawl on the ground, such as cucumbers, squash or strawberries, often become mildewed, moldy or even develop rot. A mulch prevents this damage by keeping the vegetables clean and dry.

Tests have shown that mulches sometimes support microbiological life which fights organisms deleterious to plants. Several scientists made a study of a lemon grove which almost quadrupled its yield after being mulched with wood shavings.

Since healthy root systems are associated with high citrus yields, they tried to determine what factors were involved in bringing about such an improved yield. Their approach to the problem included a study of the soil flora to determine whether there was a build-up in the mulch of some organism known to be antagonistic or parasitic to citrus root pathogens.

They found there was a fungus in the wood shavings

that parasitized two other fungi, which together or separately can cause citrus root rot, crown rot and fruit rot. Following this lead, repeated attempts were made to recover the harmful fungi from roots and soil in this mulched grove. Although the grove had a history of brown rot, the fungus was difficult to locate, indicating that it did not prosper there.

During this study of the flora in the shavings mulch, the researchers encountered other fungi which were capturing, killing and digesting free-living nematodes. Since citrus nematodes are a serious problem in many groves, the men tried to determine if these helpful fungi were capable of attacking the citrus nematode. They found that the fungi, when grown in culture and fed the larvae of the citrus nematode, readily captured and killed these root parasites.

Studies like this one have demonstrated time and again the disease fighting qualities of mulches. But a tree, shrub or plant won't get sick in the first place if it is vigorously healthy. It is most susceptible to disease when it is poorly nourished and lacking in vigor.

Avid organic orchardist Alden Stahr has demonstrated this by saving nine of the last 10 orchards he's dealt with. Stahr has moved from farm to farm, and at many of his different homes he's struggled "with remnants of old orchards, given up in past seasons as being past bearing age. But because of sentimentality, or from sheer determination," he said, "I experimented with the old trees until at last I came upon what I believe is a fountain of youth for fruit trees."

He found his discovery was similar to that of researchers at the Beltsville (Md.) Agriculture Plant Industry Station of the Department of Agriculture. In experiments there, 18-year-old apple trees with injured roots and in very poor condition made a phenomenal recovery after being mulched for two to three years with nitrogen-rich orchard hay grass.

Each tree received about 20 pounds of air dried hay, applied in June, which provided sufficient mulch to extend a foot or two beyond the spread of the branches and was about six inches in depth after being packed down by rain. No supplementary fertilizer of any kind was added to the hay-mulched trees.

High nitrogen hay mulches decompose rapidly, releasing nutrients to the roots and carbohydrates to the soil. Under these mulches, many tree roots grow in immediate contact with the decomposing hay and receive a continuous supply of nutrients. This is a dynamic process and although the mulch almost disappears each year the desirable changes have been effected.

Improvement in growth and foliage color in the Beltsville experiment was evident the year after the first application was made. Marked improvement was evident the second season; and during the third growing season after the experiment's beginning, the trees were outstandingly vigorous and productive. Unmulched trees in the same orchard location remained in poor vigor irrespective of fertilizer treatment. Trees receiving supplementary nitrogen in quantity equivalent to that supplied by the orchard grass were more vigorous than unmulched trees, but in no instance did they compare in vigor with those mulched with high-nitrogen orchard grass hay. The response to hay mulch was characterized by luxuriant dark green foliage, increased terminal and spur growths, and heavy set of fruit.

"In conjunction with our studies on tree response," the Beltsville researchers noted, "chemical analyses were made to determine the rate and total amount of the various nutrient elements released by the orchard grass mulch during the process of decomposition. These analyses showed that this mulch will provide a complete supply of nutrients for ideal growth and production, if the nitrogen content of the hay is relatively high and the rainfall adequate for decomposition and extraction."

They were orchards that were saved, but they could easily have been rose gardens or vegetable patches. Mulching makes the difference.

But mulches are more than practical—they're like frosting on the cake. While they're keeping everything beneath them cool and moist and in the proper structural relationships they're providing taste and visual appeal. Without the frosting, you still have a cake, but it isn't as good as it could be. It doesn't look as good and it doesn't taste as good. So it is with mulches. There are gardens and orchards without them, but they don't look as good as they could. Nor does the produce of unmulched orchards and gardens taste as good as it could.

Several years ago, Lewis Hill tried some experiments in hopes of coming up with a method of producing cultivated raspberries with flavor comparable to wild ones. Initially, he believed that fertilizers and soils were the keys to flavor. The principal experiment lasted several years, Hill said. It consisted, he continued, "of a dozen or so of large established Latham raspberry clumps, each of which was fertilized or mulched in a different way, to find how the different types of culture affected plant growth, and principally their influence on variances in flavor.

"In the spring, 6 clumps were treated with fertilizer as follows: (a) fresh cow manure, (b) well-age cow and horse manure, (c) finished compost, (d) dirt gathered from maple woods, (e) 5-10-10 chemical fertilizer, (f) liquid chemical fertilizer.

"Six clumps received various mulches: (g) coarse wood chips (maple), (h) sawdust (fir and spruce), (i) old hay, (j) green grass clippings, (k) maple leaves, and (l) paper mulch consisting of ordinary newspapers and magazines. The final clump, (m) received no mulch or fertilizer. None of the plants were irrigated or given additional plant food, organic or otherwise. Soil was ordinary, unimproved field soil not particularly high in humus or fertility," Hill continued.

"Results were quicker than we expected. Even the first summer there was a noticeable difference in fruit flavor, and subsequent years increased it. Since flavor cannot be measured like size or weight, and is only a matter of opinion, we called on numerous customers and visitors to our nursery to sample our berries, and compare flavor. Without knowing the details of our tests, nearly all confirmed our findings.

"The berries grown with fresh manure had a strong taste, and a handful of them together had an unpleasant smell. This was not too surprising. More than once, we had checked out complaints from customers concerning bad-flavored apples, only to find the trees had been planted near their septic tank drains!

"Berries grown with chemical fertilizers, both granular and liquid, had less fragrance, and a flat, duller taste. Well-rotted manure, woods dirt, and compost all had much better flavor and odor; but quite surprisingly ran second, in our opinion, to the mulch-grown ones," he said.

"Since the soil was not especially fertile, the quicker-rotting mulches—hay, grass, maple leaves, and paper—came closest to producing the flavor we were seeking. Soil under these mulches improved in texture much faster than in any of the other treatments, too; though in following years, those with the slower-rotting sawdust and wood chip mulch did well, falling only a little short of the others in producing vigorous plants with highly flavored fruit.

"For uniform comparison in all tests, berries were picked only when completely ripe, and nearly ready to fall off.

"The result? Mulches went on the currants, gooseberries, apples, cherries, plums, strawberries, and the rest of the raspberries. Our compost pile collected mostly garbage from then on; all else went into mulch material —like garden waste on the bottom, better-looking hay on top. Soil tilth improved vastly, staying loose and moist even during the driest part of the summer. All the trees and plants showed impressive increase in growth. Some of the young trees grew nearly twice as much in a year as before mulching, since they kept growing all season, not just after rains. Quality of fruit was much improved, too. Furthermore, now we never feel the large cultivated berries are playing second violin to any wild ones in flavor," he said.

"We found that mulching saves hard work, also. Applying mulch is certainly much easier than making and turning large compost piles, keeping them moist, and later having to work them into the soil. Now we let Nature, her bacteria, and earthworms do the job right on the spot!

"When we started our experiments, we fully expected to prove how compost produces superior flavor in berries. Instead we became convinced that to all the other arguments in favor of garden mulch, another may be added: mulching means better flavor."

Mulch means better looks, too. A mulch is visually appealing.

Picture a garden section devoted to shrub roses or other flowering perennials. In bare, uncovered soil their appeal is limited to upper levels alone. But add a layer of auburn cocoa bean hulls nestling around them, and a whole new outlook comes into view—a vista of rich color, of eye-pleasing textures and tones. Then, too, a dimension of depth completes the comfortable "carpeted" look. In bloom and out, your plants—and garden—look better right from the ground up.

Or shift the scene to the vegetable patch, where backyard eye-appeal and practical benefits go hand in hand with a cushion of thick hay or straw. Glance over to the fruit trees, which cast a far more attractive spell on the homeground horizon when they're circled with things like rough-grained bark and wood chips or ringed by a deep bed of crushed rock. And look at plantings set around the foundation of your home; invariably they fit more naturally and invitingly when a layer of pine needles, shells or leaves makes them snug.

Given a variety of mulches to work with, a gardener eager to do some "outdoor decorating" has a tool for being as creative as the fussiest of the indoor breed. At every turn of the yard and garden, mulch can help contrast the shapes and hues of plants or blossoms, highlighting backgrounds and vertical lines, or simply blending neatly with them where desirable. From a distance, the effect of certain mulches can be one that dramatically enhances any size or form of growing area. Up close, they easily perk up the mood of plant sites, transforming drab or detractive ground into handsome settings for every sort of growth.

Best of all, they prepare that handsome setting for some of the best growing you've ever seen. For while a mulch is working in the soil, sparking microbiological activity, promoting better aeration and granulation, it's working atop the soil, too. It's providing a cover to prevent the sun from baking out the moisture, creating a crust and making the land privy to runoff and erosion. It's preventing the growth of weeds and other ground cover which would compete for the moisture and nutrients in the soil. It's tempering the temperature, limiting the radical range of temperatures which beset plants.

"There is the secret", said Alden Stahr. "Mulch will do the trick. Drainage and feeding are important, but mulch is the real fountain of youth."

Or, as Mrs. Smith put it: "Our yields were fantastic. . . . so we'll again be mulching heavily . . ."

Chapter 4

MULCHING
MATERIALS

When you set out to mulch a home garden of any size, the first thing you ask is, what should I use?

There are almost as many different kinds of mulching materials as there are gardeners to use them. Mulch is a personal thing—if you ask 20 gardeners what their favorite material is and why, you may get 20 different answers. There is no one perfect mulch, but many good materials are suitable for mulching your garden. Perhaps the best way to start is to use what's easily available. There's not much sense spending hard-earned money for exotic mulches if easily found leaves will do the job you want done. Most gardeners solve their own individual gardening problems by using what is cheap and abundant locally and gets practical results for them. They have learned by experimenting to think for themselves.

Take Bob Wandzell, for example. He's a resident of Alaska where growing seasons are short and wet. Wandzell solved his gardening problems by tapping the ocean's resources. Seaweed combined with sawdust brought satisfying results in an otherwise marginal growing area.

Not long after moving to Wrangell, Alaska, Bob yearned for the fresh fruits and vegetables he had enjoyed so much in the continental United States. He decided to start his own garden. Upon checking around, he discovered that others had unsuccessfully attempted to garden in Alaska. They attributed their failure to heavy rainfall, short growing seasons, high-acid soils, non-existent local supplies of animal fertilizers, and high commercial fertilizer costs.

How did Wandzell overcome these problems to become the most successful berry and vegetable grower in southeast Alaska? Well, the first thing he did was to plot his garden on a hill, in hopes the sloped runoff would solve the excess moisture trouble. (Wrangell averages over 150 inches of rain every year.) His first garden did poorly, though—just as others had predicted. But pictures of ripe vegetables on the seed boxes, the sweat spent in preparing the patch, and the sight of weak plants struggling to mature fired up Wandell's determination and whetted his appetite for fresh produce.

The moisture problem licked, he tackled the soil deficiencies. There were no barnyard animals around Wrangell, so manure was out. He tried several commercial fertilizers without success. Then he thought waste materials from the fish canneries might do the job, but the canneries seemed to have a can for everything the fish had to offer, and there was no waste.

Finally one spring, lacking anything else to try, Wandzell mixed some seaweed—found on the beach across the street from the garden—in with his soil and planted strawberries. Late that summer the family enjoyed their fill of fresh strawberries. For some reason unknown to him, the seaweed had given the soil what it needed.

He collected five soil samples from around the garden —one of which had a high seaweed content—and sent them to the Alaska Division of Agriculture to be tested for fertilizer needs. He soon received word that four of the samples were low in phosphorus and had too high an acid content. The fifth sample, he was informed, contained everything necessary for ordinary gardening!

That fall the Wandzells gathered a large crop of seaweed that had washed ashore above the high-tide mark and dried in the sun. Wet seaweed contains 70 to 80% water—which they didn't need—so they harvested in the fall when dry weed is abundant on the beaches. They stored their ocean "crop" like hay all winter, then added it to the soil in the spring. That summer the Wandzells' garden produced the best vegetables ever grown in Wrangell.

Their rhubarb is first-class evidence of how kelp influences green leafy plants. It grows like it's trying to push back the whole Alaskan rain forest. From one short row Wandzell sold 30 to 40 pounds before the first of June last year, which is something to brag about when one considers Alaska's late springs and short growing seasons.

Even without the seaweed, sawdust makes real good

mulch, if that's what is cheap and abundant locally. Such was the case for Morton Binder. He estimated the cost of manure, peat or beanstraw and mixed the wholesale use of it in his gardening program. But he needed something to aid his rock-hard soil.

Located on a coastal plain, his soil is an extremely compacted, very fine sand over an impervious yellow clay subsoil. When he started on the yard, he began to dig a post-hole and thought he had hit a rock. Even a pick refused to chip off more than bite-sized chunks. He filled the hole with water and the next day had to bail it out to continue digging.

Then he remembered that in a nursery where he had worked a lot of old shavings from the sawdust bins had been used. "A lumber mill is close by," Binder explained. "I went up to look over the situation. There were literally thousands of yards of coarse mill sawdust chips free for the taking. I carried sufficient back with me in a few trips to heap a foot deep over the entire future garden area. The deep surface mulch held the irrigation water without runoff, and within two or three days the fine sand was ready to spade. It took three times over to get a good mix. This could have been done much more simply with a hand tractor, but it was in an inaccessible position," he explained.

The upshot of his labors was a better soil. He said it became "increasingly friable and plants are responding well." He continued, "I ran a pH on the sawdust and found it to be 4.5, or about that of peat moss. In an alkaline soil this would be fine, but in my 5.5–6 soil I had to add lime.

"Weeds pull readily when the soil is mulched with

sawdust. The water bill has been negligible, even though our water rates are high. Humidity is maintained at all times. The ground looks and feels good, and caking is a thing of the past. Cultivation has been reduced to minimum and the angleworms are becoming more prevalent," he said.

"The amount of manure, organic matter, and lime used was no greater than if I had been working with a friable soil in the first place. I estimate my total soil-

Sawdust, available free from the lumber yard, is one of the most inexpensive soil builders.

building cost at two gallons of gas, although it did take a lot of hard work," he concluded.

Another sawdust mulcher, Mary Leister, reaped similar benefits with a similar outlay. She was able to get sawdust to mulch her garden "at the expenditure only of time and physical effort." Unlike the variety Binder used, however, Mrs. Leister's sawdust was well rotted from having spent 20 years lying in a shady woods.

"This sawdust was," she explained, "moist and very heavy to handle, but its dark color was most pleasing to the eye. Even the lightest of rains seemed to go directly through to the garden soil and very little additional water was needed throughout the summer by the herbaceous annuals and perennials protected by it, nor did they show any overt need for additional fertilizers during the growing season. The vegetable garden grew lushly, and strawberries, raspberries and rhubarb all produced prodigiously surrounded and protected by this sawdust mulch.

"No replenishing of the mulch was necessary from spring to fall," she continued. "Not one garden weed penetrated the three inches of sawdust, and only an amazing few of the broken roots of the creeping woods plants gave rise to new growth that had to be pulled from the loose, unresisting medium.

"On the same July day when the soil beneath the dried grass registered 94 degrees F., that beneath the rotted sawdust registered only 82 degrees. These temperature readings were taken in the same test bed, in the same direct rays of the sun, and within four feet of each other.

"In early November, checking the decomposition

and/or loss of the sawdust, I found approximately two inches of loose mulching material, while the first inch or so of soil immediately beneath was so mixed with the sawdust as to be inseparable one from the other. It was, in effect, a rich, black, moist soil, brought about, probably, by the action of rain water, soil bacteria, and little earth animals," she said.

Mrs. Leister, in the course of her gardening, has had the opportunity to try some other mulch materials. She approached her mulching endeavors with these other materials with the same observant care she applied to her test of rotten sawdust. The others she tried were grass clippings, a material available to anyone with a lawn; shredded pine bark, a commercially-available mulch, and ground cork, a relatively little-used mulch. Each was spread on the Leister garden and "checked for its desirability as a mulch."

"Our lawn, green, healthy and practically devoid of weeds, has always provided a more than abundant supply of clippings to cover, thin layer by thin layer, every bed and border in our garden," she said. The pale gray-green color of the drying grass deepens to brown and is not unpleasant. It readily permits raindrops to penetrate to the soil beneath, while its decomposition enriches the soil, and its shady protection keeps the earth beneath it both cooler and damper than cultivated soil exposed to the elements. On a day in July when the air temperature was 98 degrees F. and the temperature, in direct sunlight, at the surface of the mulch registered 120, the surface of the soil beneath the dried grass mulch was 94 degrees.

"These grass clippings, however, require almost

weekly replenishment in order to keep the mulching depth a preferred 3 inches. This rapid decomposition necessitates the constant addition of organic fertilizers rich in nitrogen, to the soil; and the protected plants, even in a season of fairly normal rainfall, are very often in need of additional moisture. Furthermore, by freeze-up time very little dried grass is ever left for use as a winter mulch," she continued.

"One of the most striking things about shredded pine bark," she explained, "is the woodsy fragrance that rises when the bark is spread. It is," she said, "so heavenly that the gardener is apt to feel that even if its mulching capabilities are nil it is worth its price in nostril-tingling value alone. But, fortunately for the garden, it is an excellent mulch. Its pine-woods aroma vanishes after a few weeks' exposure to the elements, but its dark color remains pleasing to the eye for at least the two years I have used it," she reported.

"It does not rob the soil of moisture but instead appears to allow every falling drop to penetrate to the earth. Its fine, dusty particles are, of course, quickly absorbed by the soil, but this is such an extremely small percentage of the mulch that its disappearance is scarcely noted, either in the depth of the mulch on the ground or in the bulk recovered if it is raked up for storage during the winter months. The dust absorbed presumably increases, to a slight degree, the acidity of the soil, but does not noticeably increase the demand for nitrogen.

"Possibly because the larger pieces and consequent greater unevenness of the shredded pine bark mulch allow some moisture to escape, but more likely because the foundation planting suffers from being in the rain shadow of the house, a considerable amount of additional moisture was required by these large evergreens. So, too, the smaller-rooted cuttings in the test bed required a great deal of additional water, but this need not necessarily be laid at the door of the pine bark mulch."

She continued, "When the surface temperature of this mulch was 120 degrees F., the temperature of the soil directly beneath it was 86 degrees, while a temperature of 90 degrees was registered in medium shade with the soil beneath it registering 82 degrees F.

"The other mulching material tested was ground cork—not yet, to my knowledge, on the open market.

"This material was so light and so easy to handle that a 90-pound woman could spread it with ease. It was also so light that I feared the first breeze would blow it across the countryside and that even the moderate force of an ordinary raindrop would dislodge it from place. But I was wrong.

"Scarcely had we spread this mulch when an early-summer thunderstorm raced across the land," she said. "Preceded by violent winds, it let loose a volley of pounding, outsize raindrops, and then sluiced down veritable waterfalls upon the earth. The storm passed, the sun shone, and we went out to view the end of the mulch test that had not yet fairly begun; and there lay the ground cork, smoothly and evenly spread upon the ground, completely unruffled by either wind or water. The cork itself was damp, the ground beneath it soaked, and from that moment through the entire growing season that section of the test garden relied solely on nature for its watering.

"This ground cork is reported, authoritatively, to test one per cent nitrogen, a fairly negligible amount; but its deterioration is so unbelievably slow that it appears almost to be an inert material and its effect for good or ill on the nitrogen content of the soil is not observable except probably by highly scientific testing methods. Measured by bulk, there appears to be exactly as much cork in November as there was in May.

"Well known for its insulating qualities, there should be no surprise that where its surface registered the same 120 degrees F. mentioned before, the temperature of the surface of the soil directly beneath was 82 degrees; and in light shade where the mulch surface showed 94 degrees, the soil beneath showed 78 degrees F.," she said.

"Dry or wet it is completely odorless. Its only drawback—and it is no doubt quibbling to mention it in view of its other excellences—is its pale-tan color which does not enhance the beauty of a planting as a darker color would do."

If a pale tan color is a drawback, you'd never know from listening to hay mulchers. These gardeners spread that pale tan substance over, around and through their gardens with nary a thought that it should be darker to best enhance the garden. For Fred Eaton, for example, hay mulching has too many practical advantages for him to be concerned about whether its color appeals to him. He's been using a hay-mulch for years and finds it a fine labor-saver.

"Make the right start in hay-mulch gardening by making the best choice of the hay itself," he recommended. "*Make every effort to get baled hay.* It's neater, and is much easier to manage than loose hay. It's a better weed smotherer, and stays in place even in high spring winds.

"Don't depend on a mulch for a complete soil nutrient provider" he continued. "It's main value, after decomposition, is as a soil conditioner. It does contain some nutrient value, however, so try to get it organically-grown, if possible. Well-fed hay will return a greater percentage of nutrients to your soil and crops. A rich and early-cut grass hay often contains more nutrient value than a starved clover or alfalfa.

"Before you start to mulch, apply fertilizer in the usual way as you always do. Compost, manures, rock powders, and other organic materials will tend to decompose more quickly under a cooling, moisture-holding hay mulch, so even if you've never tried surface fertilizing (or sheet composting) before, don't be afraid to try it now. We don't hesitate to use lots of phosphate rock, granite stone meal (good for potash and mineral supply), and a magnesium limestone (only when needed to raise pH.) This general fertilizing program is far from scientific, but it works wonders with plants, probably because, unlike chemicals, it is 'nature-balanced' in its original form. All the many trace minerals lacking in straight chemical formulas are present in almost every organic and rock fertilizer," Eaton continued.

It should be pointed out that such a program of fertilizing is the best, regardless of the nature of mulch you use. But there are some pitfalls in using unrotted organic materials and planting at the same time. These are explained in chapter seven.

"Fertilizing over and done, let's start to plant. Again, there is nothing special here, and you may proceed to plant as you have always done," he explained. "First drop in or sow your first row of seeds. Then go to your bale of hay, and peel off a two-inch layer 'book.' Place it alongside of the seed row. Continue peeling off books, until the entire row is flanked by straw. Then repeat this process on the other side of the row. A medium to large field-baled bale should cover about 40 feet of row. Now, if you'll stand back and look at the results of your efforts, you'll see a newly-planted row of seed running parellel in between hay books, laid end to end. Who said mulching is untidy?

"Your second seed row should be placed just outside of the second row of books you laid for the first row. Confused? Just lay out seed rows and place one row of books between each seed row.

"By midsummer, the hay should be pretty well on the way to decomposition, and the books should have been compressed to half their original thickness. By this time, some weeds and grass will have fought their way through the hay. There's no need to hand-weed, however. This is the time to apply a second layer right on top of the first. In late autumn, while closing out the garden season, you should re-cover any bare or thin spots in the mulch rows.

"Next year, you'll really reap all the benefits of this system. Take a rake or a potato hook, and pull the remaining mulch to one side for a distance of half a book width, so that you expose the ground for a planting row right in the middle of where the path or row of hay was before. Get it? You are now to plant in the richest area, that was the middle of your mulch strip last year. And you are covering last year's row space to kill weeds and grass, and make rich soil for a third year," Eaton said.

"You'll find it unnecessary to dig or cultivate this ground before seeding. It will be loose, rich, humus-full, and abounding with earthworms. Just loosen enough ground with the corner of a hoe to get your seed in to proper depth, cover, and tamp. From now on, Mother Nature takes over many of your former duties.

"With this system," Eaton said, "we don't have to cultivate any more. We don't water, except in extreme drought; we do no weeding except at the first thinning or transplanting of the seedlings. Because we applied our minerals (granite dust and phosphate rock) liberally at first, we haven't been adding any fertilizing materials either.

"Only two and a half years of the book system has converted our depleted, packed, humus-lacking soil into a rich, soft, mellow garden that certainly does grow good vegetables. And this land has probably been used and abused for over 250 years.

"In only three years, we have seen our soil consistently in tilth and productivity. The hay mulch, constantly in contact with the soil, not only gives us the usual advantages of a mulch (which would be reason enough to use it), but actually conditions the soil with practically no effort on our part," Eaton said.

Another gardener who believes in a good hay mulch is John Krill. His garden is constantly covered with a mulch of old hay, weeds, straw and leaves. The mulch must be constantly renewed, however, because decomposition reduces its depth quickly. The Ohioan decided that the best way to handle the renewal was "to grow my mulch right where I wanted it. That would be right over the mulch already spread out over the garden. I bought a bushel of oats and sowed them by broadcasting over the brown mulch," he explained. "Oats are cheap and a bushel sows one heck of a big area. I scattered the oats thickly because I wanted a good and heavy stand.

"What happened? I noticed next day that a few sparrows were gorging on the oats. So what? What could a few tiny birds do to all those oats scattered out there? Next day there were more, and on each succeeding day their numbers increased until I felt sure there were more birds than oats in the garden. I looked skyward for some signs of rain. A good wetting would cause the oats to sprout quickly with the sprouts preventing the birds from eating them. No rain. And very quickly there were no oats," he continued.

"When the rains came much later, the few handfuls of oats that had worked down out of reach deep in the mulch sprouted. They grew lushly, relishing the cool weather. But as I had planned, they never matured. Winter stormed over the land and the tender oats were killed by continuing freezing temperatures.

"The blades that had stood up so erectly were now flat on the surface of the mulch. Snow came and buried them. When spring arrived and the snow had vanished, I found a thick layer of flattened oat blades. This much of my idea had worked. I was determined to beat the birds the following fall. I used two methods, both of them good. Both are practical and may be used almost anywhere that oats will grow. Oats like cool weather, hence for this purpose must be seeded in the fall.

"The following autumn turned out to be nearly as dry. It seemed to me the birds were already gathering in anticipation of more free oats. I did broadcast the oats, but the birds did not disturb them. There was one prime difference in them this time.

"I had emptied the oats into a tub. Then I poured enough water over them to give them a good soaking. The tub was covered with burlap and placed in a cool, shady place. A garage or cellar provides ideal conditions for this purpose. Everyday I would stir the damp oats, adding water if they appeared to be drying out," Krill said.

"Then the oats showed signs of sprouting. I kept watering and stirring them to keep rot from setting in. Finally the tub was a tangle of greenish-white oat sprouts. When they were two or more inches long, I waited until evening and then broadcast them over the garden. True, the birds did come down and searched out every grain that they could swallow. But these were grains that had not sprouted for some reason. Those with the sprouts they left alone.

"The sprouts fell in every nook and cranny in the not yet compacted mulch. The blades turned a healthy green and shot upward rapidly. Late September became late October and the sprouts thickly covered the garden with a sturdy growth. But before the blades could set their heads of seed, the constantly intensifying cold slowly withered them.

"Snow buried the fallen oats. The weight of the snow, plus the hard beating of a number of rains flattened them flush with the mulch out of which they grew. Spring found my garden already mulched with mulch right in place.

"I seeded oats by a second method without going through the process of sprouting them. It is equally good and equally simple to use. I had quite a quantity of old hay which was to be spread in the garden as mulch. Again you must wait until late September or the early weeks of October to use oats.

"I broadcast the oats thickly over the garden. (I must add that sprouting the oats will not interfere with gathering any vegetables which may be growing up until a killing frost arrives.) Over the scattered oats I spread the hay. It makes little difference how thickly the mulch is applied, for by the time it has compacted, the oats will have sprouted through it," he continued.

"This method also defied the birds, for they could not poke deep enough in the protective mulch cover to reach the grains. A rain soaked the garden thoroughly and in a few days spears of green wove a mosiac over the brown mulch. Once started, the oats grew with a gratifying abandon. Soon they were so thick that the mulch could scarcely be seen.

"Before they could head, winter destroyed them and they fell wilted to the mulch, adding themselves to it. Again snows and rains beat the blades flat. Spring came and the garden was a mat of flattened and dense oat grasses that covered the original mulch," Krill concluded.

Krill liked the results of his experiment. Years later, he's still using the method. But one man's passion is another's poison, or at least not his passion. Lee Shields, an Indiana resident, uses another material for his mulch, a material abundant locally, and one he doesn't have to plant. Shields uses old leaves. He gets them from the city during each year's fall cleanup.

The city street department dumps from two to four truckloads on his garden each year when they are removing them from the streets in his neighborhood—all free. This may sound like a tremendous amount of leaves, but since they are wet when dumped by the trucks they immediately start to "heat" and break down. By the following summer, the "mountains" of leaves have been reduced to about one-third of the original bulk. He does not "turn" the piles—they are only handled once. (Other gardeners find that wet leaves tend to "wad" up into layers and resist bacterial action unless stirred and turned occasionally.)

Each year he takes leaves directly from the piles that were heaped up the previous fall, and works them into the soil to steadily improve its tilth and structure. Such application is usually made before the dry, hot summer days set in, preserving valuable growing moisture.

Shields likes to cultivate at least once before applying mulch, and give the soil a chance to warm up well. Then, a heavy application is made right up close to the plants, which will also help prevent them from blowing over during wind and rainstorms. By the following spring, most of the leaves are decayed enough so the rotary tiller effectively incorporates them with the soil.

Using leaf mulches is practical for the gardener since the supply is generally boundless in most communities. And it's practical for the community, which usually doesn't know what to do with its boundless supply of leaves. In most areas, the leaves are simply burned, which wastes good mulch and puts more smoke into air which doesn't need it.

Waste is the key. Most mulches are waste, to everyone but the mulcher. Dave Shaw uses wood chips, for example. Wood chips would be a waste material to most people, but to Shaw they're nutrients in his soil.

Like Shields, Shaw, a southern New Jersey resident, likes to thoroughly turn his old mulch and sod into the soil each spring.

When first planting a new section of his garden that formerly was sod, Shaw goes back and forth with the

Wood chip mulch retains moisture, controls weeds and creates handsome background for rhododendron plant.

tiller about four times, working it down to about eight inches deep. He then applies a new four-inch layer of chips, adding cottonseed meal and dried chicken manure at the same time. Shaw tried mulching without tilling to break up new ground prior to planting, but discovered it took longer to eliminate weeds and grasses.

At spring planting time, Shaw moves the chips aside, makes a furrow with the hoe, drops in the seed, covers and tamps. As the plants grow, the chips are replaced around them. After crops are harvested in fall, the entire garden area gets several truckloads of chips to maintain the 4-inch depth.

When growing potatoes, Shaw plants them in about 12 inches of chips and straw, pressing the seed into the soil surface. Clean potatoes are picked merely by separating chips and breaking them off plants.

Although for most plants it makes no difference what kind of wood is used, Shaw does apply only pine chips and pine needles to his strawberry rows because of their acid reaction. Ordinary chips are close enough to neutral to cause no problem. The only potential problem with the constant chip mulch is an occasional nitrogen deficiency, evident when foliage begins to yellow. When this happens, Shaw applies cottonseed or bone meal, but, he said, "As long as you keep the chips above ground and don't mix them with the soil, you don't have nitrogen deficiency."

Shaw is proud of the lawn-building job he did at his Godparents' home along the Jersey shore. The soil there was just sand and gravel when he applied 3 inches of chips and 2 inches of old chicken manure. He worked the mixture in well before planting. "Now that lawn is one of few in the area to have done so well with so little extra care."

He actually has sold so many people on the advantages of chips that "there's almost not enough to go around for everybody who wants to use the chips." In fact, he's glad to have his own chopper. Whenever his supply from tree-trimming crews gets low, he can always make his own chips from his farm's timber supply.

Shaw's primary source of the wood chips is a good source of mulching material for anyone: tree trimming operations. Utility companies and many cities have crews which annually trim branches which overhang their wires and other overhead facilities.

Ohio Edison Company, for example, does this. Instead of burning tree limbs that have been cut down, the Ohio Edison crews put them into chipping machines that shred leaves and limbs alike into small bits of material. This matter, when it decomposes, makes excellent mulch and top dressing. And Ohio Edison gives it away.

The leaves in the material contribute the most to its decomposition. They break down first and help to decompose the bits of wood, a process that does not occur quickly.

Archer Martin got a pile of the material in July. For several weeks it smelled like new ensilage and continued to be warm for two and a half months, showing that decomposition still was occurring. He expected that by the next summer they would be broken down completely and would do much to improve the consistency of the soil. Meanwhile, he used some of the material to protect his roses and other perennials over the winter.

"I did not give the chips any special treatment," Martin explained, "merely piling them in a mound with a depression at the top to catch rainfall. I wet down the pile frequently during dry periods and added wood ashes and grass cuttings atop it for no other reason than that the pile was a convenient place to put them. (To be truly effective, the ashes should have been mixed through the pile when I built it. I shall do that before I use it.)"

Ervin Steinmetz, an Ohio Edison tree foreman, has used the shredded material for winter protection of his

Utility company shredders quickly convert sawed-off limbs and leaves into free-for-the-asking mulch.

roses. He applied it after frost, though, and then spaded it into the soil early the next spring. The mulch shouldn't be put down while still green during the growing season, for it will rob the plants of nitrogen during its decomposition.

A farmer who lives near Steinmetz has been allowing the Ohio Edison Company to dump as many chips as it wants into an old gravel pit on his farm, with the idea in mind that he eventually will use the decomposed material for top dressing his fields.

Ohio Edison considers the use of chippers to be more economical than the old practice of piling whole limbs on trucks to be hauled away.

The utility firm almost always has men clearing limbs away from its lines during the growing season. If they are working in particularly heavy growth, they will fill a truck with shredded matter every hour or so. They haul the stuff to dumps, or to nurserymen and farmers who can use it in unlimited quantities.

The hauling, however, takes time and costs money, so Ohio Edison people are pleased when someone—usually a gardener—comes with truck or trailer to where the men are working and asks for the material. If your utility firm, whether electric or telephone, does not use chippers, a suggestion to the management might open up a new supply of free mulch for your community's gardeners.

And while you're checking the utilities, try calling other local industries, such as lumberyards, milling firms or food processing firms. Mulch is where you find it, and a little scouting around is generally worth the effort.

According to Robert Mead, thousands of tons of sawdust and shavings are used each year as bedding for the booming dairy industry in Vermont, for example. In addition to the natural fertilizer value of the sawdust and shavings, they absorb much of the fertilizer value from the cow manure that would otherwise be lost. Some mills gladly give this away to get it out of their way. At others there is a charge, a common cost being one cent a bushel. Some shavings are baled, with the usual price being 50 to 75 cents a bale.

Many other wood by-products are freely or cheaply available for use as mulch. In addition to the sawdust and wood chips and shavings that have already been mentioned, one can use bark and packing materials, such as shredded paper or excelsior. Peat moss, too, is good mulch.

The by-products of your own or others' gardening activities can be used as mulch. Use those weeds for mulch. And the grass clippings, pine needles, rotted pine wood, corn cobs and stalks and tobacco stems.

In Kentucky, for example, the tobacco remedy is the first thing people think of when their lawns are doing poorly. If it works for them, it should for anyone who has access to the tobacco stems. The remedy is really a mulch of tobacco stems. After the last leaves are raked in the fall, the Kentuckians spread a thick layer of tobacco stems over the lawn. Winter rains and snows leach the nutrients from the stalks into the soil. In the spring, the stalks are raked up. The tobacco farmers themselves use the stalks in some areas, usually tilling them into the soil.

In corn country, widely-used mulches are corn cobs

and corn stalks. Ground into one-inch bits, the cobs have many uses. The sugar content of them will benefit the microorganisms in the soil and will promote better soil granulation. Shredded corn stalks—provided the stalks weren't infested with borers—make a well-aerated winter mulch.

In the southern states, rice hulls, cotton burrs and hulls and pecan and peanut shells are readily available as mulch materials. Most of these materials are rich in nitrogen and potash. They are unusually attractive as a mulch, too. If you happen to live in the northern areas of the country, you may find the nut shells available commercially.

If you live near a brewery, check the availability of spent hops and grain used in the beer-making process. These are good as mulch.

Gardeners in Florida and Georgia often use excess hyacinth plants as mulch. The plants abound in these states. They can be used as is or ground to a pulp.

It all depends, again, on what is cheaply and abundantly available locally. In the Canary Islands, to use a far off example, an old custom, dating back 100 years or more, is to mulch with picon, which are small volcanic pebbles. Picon farming, as it is called, is a variation on stone mulching, which is covered more fully in the next chapter. Its biggest advantage, according to practitioners, is that it conserves, as do most mulches, fertilizer and water, both in short supply on the barren islands.

The custom dates back to the last major volcanic eruption in the islands. When they could get back to their homes, the farmers found their fields covered with volcanic rock. But it was planting time, and they could do nothing else but dig holes through the pebbles and plant. To their amazement, they had record crops that year and in subsequent years developed the following procedure of protecting the ground with the small pebbles left by the lava flow.

First, furrows are cleared away, and animal manure placed in the soil is covered over, and a top layer of from one to three inches of picon is put on. The row is watered, and when it seasons well, it is planted through holes made in the picon for insertion of seeds or seedlings.

Farmers say a picon covering can be left undisturbed for 20 to 30 years, with only small additions of fertilizer needed from time to time, put in through the holes in the picon at planting time. Watering is unnecessary, for the picon not only holds in what moisture there is, but collects additional moisture from the atmosphere during the short rainy and foggy seasons, and stores it in the ground below. Weeding is minimal, another saving in time and labor.

Chief beneficiaries of the picon treatment are cactus farms, which produce sisal fibers for rope and cochineal insects for carmine and like dyes. But without picon, home gardeners would find it impossible to grow tomatoes, corn, melons, cucumbers, squash or potatoes.

Without a somewhat similar material, Ruth Bixler would have found it impossible to keep her flowers growing. Mrs. Bixler had had tremendous problems keeping anything growing in the shaley soil at her Pennsylvania home. An intensive mulch program saved her vegetable patch and stone mulches—explained in the next chapter—saved her trees. Nothing worked for her flowers, however, until she discovered and tried a picon-like material.

"One Saturday," she explained, "I stopped at the feed store to get some feed for our pet rabbit, and right in front of me I saw the answer—bags of ground oyster shell. I bought bag after bag and started shaking it over the beds. I really put it on thick and it was beautiful for the summer; not even a heavy shower disturbed it.

"To my surprise the few weeds that came up pulled right out as if the ground underneath was wet. It cut my weeding time down to once a month (before that every week). The roses were never more beautiful and bloomed until the first snow. I also used it thick on my Mimosa trees and they got through the severe winter without a single loss."

What this all means is that to succeed in the mulching system of gardening, you have to be what Owen M. Voigt calls a "pack rat." He figures that's what he is. Voigt has toured and explored Virginia's Shenandoah Valley countless times in search of mulch materials for his garden.

"I have become an expert in our county's various industries, have memorized hundreds of miles of scenic back roads, and have made the acquaintance of many interesting people," he said. "I now feel I am truly a citizen—almost a native—of the area to which we migrated several years ago.

"Luckily, mulching poses the need for more common sense than funds, so we were able to utilize our limited resources to good advantage. The nooks and corners where our search for material took us were fascinating, and in the long run as educational and rewarding as the improvement wrought by our horticultural endeavors.

"People everywhere were considerate of our needs. They recognized the basic common sense behind our methods, and were always ready to give us what we needed.

"When I visited a furniture factory for sawdust, the manager took me on a tour of inspection and showed me the sawdust pile which loomed imposingly in an

Shredded pine bark mulch around fruit trees holds in moisture, promotes new root growth.

adjacent field. But he pointed out that it was an overfine residue of many woodworking operations and was prone to cake. He suggested a local sawmill which cuts logs and rough lumber—much better for my uses. I located the mill which was operated part-time by a genial farmer. Here, for just a few cents, I was able to acquire large amounts of good red oak sawdust— enough to mulch my lengthy 500-foot hedge, and to add to my compost heap.

"However, my farmer-sawmill operator passed me on to another and larger mill which uses a debarker system on their logs. They gave me a very generous amount of shredded bark, which I found to be the most successful evergreen mulch I have tried," Voigt said.

"The soil beneath an inch or slightly more of this shredded bark never showed signs of extreme drying, although we had some very hot suns during the severe droughts. Through it all, the shrubs retained a healthy deep green, while the soil, unrobbed of nutrients and nitrogen, was alive with beneficial insects, fungi and earth worms. I would also like to add that it gives a very professional finish to your vegetable rows and ornamental beds and borders, very pleasing to the eye, while it keeps the weeds down rigorously.

"In the fall of the year, trucks of the sanitation department roam the streets collecting huge piles of leaves with a suction pump. I contacted the chief engineer of the town waste disposal system who told me they were dumped on a public fill project, and were available to all who chose to collect them. Here indeed was a bonanza overlooked by almost all of the local horticulturists, many of whom still burn their leaves. The action of the pump in sucking up the leaves grinds them up into a powder, so I was able to collect close to a ton easily. Last year when I made the mistake of spreading them in the spring, the ground was very slow in heating up. So this year I plowed them under in the fall, letting the now-abundant worms and bacteria consume them through the winter."

As Voigt toured the valley looking for mulch materials, he also kept his eyes open for organic fertilizers. "I consider a large supply of burlap bags in the car's trunk an absolute necessity," he said. "It's also advantageous, I find, to keep a small notebook which lists places and areas cited by friendly advisers as possible sources for more and different organic complements.

"Trouble, and time-consuming? Yes, I guess it is if you mark down each moment to drudgery. But what are adventures into the back roads and bypassed nooks of your community? And what is that pioneer's satisfaction that comes with building a really fine garden from a square of waste soil? Is this trouble, is it pleasure, or is it achievement?

"Two years ago, local gardeners considered my methods a little nutty—to say the least. But this fall I caught my neighbor quietly sneaking in a load of leaves to cover his garden.

"It looks as if being a pack rat is contagious!"

Chapter Five

STONE MULCHING

When "Pack rat" Owen Voigt first started roaming the Shenandoah Valley in search of mulching materials, one of his first specific desires was stones—big ones, little ones, round ones, jagged ones—just stones.

"If you have never used a rock mulch," he said, "I heartily recommend it." For Voigt, a big factor was that rocks aren't too hard to find and are used just as they are found. All he had to do was find a rock, plunk it in place and he had mulch. Moreover, rocks are free.

Rock mulching is pretty much like every other kind of mulching. Rocks do everything that other mulches do. In some instances, they do it better. They are, for example, exceptionally good for conserving moisture and moderating daily temperature fluctuations and particularly good at maintaining soil structure. And when was the last time you saw a weed sprout through a stone?

Most any vegetation can be stone mulched, but it works particularly well for trees and it looks particularly good with flowers and other decorative vegetation. L. T. Servais, a Green Bay, Wisconsin, gardener and rock collector, uses his functional stone mulches to show off his collection.

"I have been using rock mulches around fruit trees for 20 years now with good results," he said. "As a rock collector, I at first kept my collection of specimens from a dozen states and Canada in the house. But when they really began to get in the way, cluttering up closets,

A mulch of rocks combines neatness with moisture conservation while it discourages weeds.

shelves and cabinets, I moved them outdoors and put them to work around my trees. I have replaced the more drab stones now with rose quartz, gleaming obsidian, and shining feldspar to add a bit of glamour to my tree plantings while helping them to grow better."

While a rock mulch's ability to make a garden look better might be a matter of opinion, its ability to make plants grow better appears to be a historical fact. Evidence of stone mulching in ancient Rome has been found in the writings of Virgil, the great Roman poet. His agricultural directives included the following instructions:

"Finally, put your rooted grape cuttings firmly down in the ground, be sure to add sufficient earth and sprinkle rich manure over it. Also dig in some stones, perhaps pumice, perhaps rounded sea shells; for, between these, water will seep down and the air will gently penetrate and inspire growth in your plants. I have even found some who loaded heavy fieldstones on top or considerable weights of broken pots; this is protection against cloudbursts and against the hot summer heat which cracks the thirsty fields."

Columella, who was the best prose writer on agriculture in Roman times, related that stones were placed even between the roots. Similar practices prevailed in olive groves. The olives like lime stones particularly. The olive was planted in trenches four feet deep into which it was the custom to deposit stones for encouraging moisture around the roots.

Stone mulching has been used to great advantage on the Organic Gardening Experimental Farm. Author and publisher J. I. Rodale did quite a bit of successful experimenting with stone mulches.

"Somewhere in the 1940's," he wrote some years ago, "I got the idea of growing vegetables in a stone garden, with alternate layers of soil and stone . . . For almost 20 years we have planted vegetables in this garden with excellent results. It seems that something about the stones communicates itself into the plants to make them grow faster and be healthy . . .

"The one bad feature of this kind of a garden was that the weeds would grow between the stones and could not be cleaned out as with a weeding tool in a conventional garden. They would have to hand-picked. So one day . . . while my wife Anna and I stood looking at a stone section overgrown with weeds, she observed, 'Perhaps if we would put another layer of stones over the existing ones, it would be more difficult for the weeds to poke their way through them.' No sooner said than done."

That experiment turned out to be as successful as the original test of the stone-mulched garden itself. Rodale reported some of the more unusual and unexpected benefits of rock mulching. It is, for example, a good method of plowless farming, that is, farming in which the upper layer of soil isn't disturbed. He reported that plowing can be used, but that it isn't necessary to plow deeply. In the spring, the upper four or five inches of soil is merely stirred about a bit before seeding. This stirring is easy because the earth is soft and moist between the stones. If some organic fertilizer is being used, the shallow plowing keeps it close to the surface where it will be more accessible to oxygen and will decay faster.

"A stone mulch causes the earth under it to be well-aerated, usually more so than exposed soil, strange as it may seem," he wrote. "You can verify this by merely looking at a stone resting above the soil. The rain causes a shallow channel to form in the soil under the outer rim of each rock, permitting air to enter, whereas the baking action of the sun on exposed soil and blowing of wind over it harden the surface into crusts that can be lifted up bodily.

"The conditions under stones are ideal for bacteria, earthworms and other burrowing insects," he continued. "A dampened darkness prevails that is favorable for the working of bacteria and beneficial insects.

"Groves of sickly limes, citrus trees and other fruits have been revived when rocks were piled high around the trunks to help keep the bark from scorching and the roots from becoming dry and hot. The vigor and growth of both ornamental and fruit orchard trees is increased by rock mulching when teamed with sound organic care. Consistently better yields and quality of plums, peaches, apples and cherries have been reported by many gardeners and farmers using the rock-mulch system. Young fruit trees have been especially benefited in getting a strong start," he wrote.

Margaret L. Wood is a stone mulcher whose experience with the system tested it to an extreme. She had read about the system and its results at the Organic Gardening Experimental Farm and elsewhere. She viewed it as something of a last resort. Mrs. Wood and her family live in Arizona's Mojave Desert. Since every drop of water used by the Woods, their dogs and cats, horse, cattle and sheep and their plants must be trucked in, the moisture conserving qualities of a good rock mulch were on the line.

"We took possession of our new home in a July following an unusually wet period in May and June," Mrs. Wood explained. "The trees and shrubs were green and lovely. Then the weather returned to normal. In Arizona that means *hot* and *dry*. The ground baked until a hoe just bounced off it, and you couldn't dig a hole without first soaking it for an hour or so. Hauling water became a daily, not weekly chore, but even so the shrubs and shade trees drooped and shed most of their leaves. The tips of branches on the fruit trees died back. The evergreens looked limp and actually seemed to shrink. Everything wilted, including us. The situation looked hopeless," she said.

Then she remembered Rodale's stone mulch. "If there was any one thing we had lots of on our desert land it was rocks—big rocks, little rocks, granite, quartz, turquoise, sandstone, limestone—we had them all. From then on, every morning and evening, and even some afternoons, found the children and me out hauling rocks in a wheelbarrow and garden cart. Judging by the expressions on their faces as they drove by, the neighbors must have been pretty certain that the sun had gone to our heads.

"The first thing we tackled was the shrubs and bedding plants against the west side of the house. Afternoons they were broiling and mornings, when it was shady, the seven kittens were literally tearing them to bits. We gave the whole bed a quick overall cover of fist-sized rocks which the contractor had obligingly left pushed up nearby, soaked the covered bed for a couple

Stones in a rainbow of colors prove mulch can be decorative as well as protective.

of hours with a sprinkler hose turned upside down, and as simply as that the flowers and bushes stopped dying and actually began to grow. A few even bloomed. Now don't misunderstand me. I didn't say that suddenly we had a lovely flower bed. This was still the desert in July and the soil in the spot was hard and barren, but these plants were now at least holding their own, and they continued to do so if watered lightly with the sprinkler hose once a week," she continued.

"By now it was obvious that the foundation planting in the front (the east side) was losing its battle with the dogs and the heat, so we worked on it next. We were now able to scrape up a few wheelbarrow loads of manure in the corral, so we could do a more thorough rescue job here.

"First we made a manure dike a foot high, a foot across, and 18 inches from the plants the full length of the beds and across the ends. This was then shored up on both sides with the biggest rocks we could manage to get into the wheelbarrow. The top of the dike was covered with smaller rocks to keep it from weathering away.

"When we had finished, the two beds in front had become, in effect, two rock-bottomed reservoirs bounded on two sides by the manure-rock dikes and on the other two by the foundation and the cement steps," she explained. "We filled them with water to a depth of eight to 10 inches and let it soak into the ground, and these bushes grew and flowered and the little pyracantha set a full crop of large, well-colored berries.

"Again, this was no lovely flower bed. These were small shrubs two to three feet apart, and partially hidden this first year by the big rocks—but they grew, despite the heat, on only one watering a month from then on.

"Our next project was the rhubarb and shrubs along the north side of the house. They received the same treatment, and the rhubarb continued to send up new growth all summer," Mrs. Wood continued.

"By this time our backs were stronger and our manure pile bigger, and we decided to see what we could do for the trees, grapevines, and rose bushes which were too widely separated for that sort of treatment. Since we had finally run out of readily available rocks, we began by building circular manure dikes two to three feet from the tree trunks, wetting them down with the hose and letting them "bake" in the hot sun. These were then filled to the top with water every 10-14 days and the trees began to grow. Some of the Scotch pines grew more than a foot through August and September, and later the fruit trees began forming blossom buds for spring. The roses appeared blighted or diseased, so they were pruned back almost to the ground after diking, then responded with fresh, healthy new growth and a few perfect blossoms for Christmas.

"Meanwhile, we hauled in rocks whenever we could. As each tree was rocked up, a six to eight inch layer of trash from around the hay stack was placed between the tree trunk and the dike to make it easier to tuck in sprigs of myrtle and sweet alyssum and a few bulbs here and there," she said.

It took muscle, some perseverance and lots of a cheap and locally abundant material—rock—but the Woods finally got their little chunk of the desert blooming like an oasis. And it wasn't a mirage, either.

Another stone mulcher is Georgia Montfort. She didn't find herself in a do-or-die situation such as the Woods. For her it was a matter of developing a rock garden for show and watching—somewhat amazed—as her plants slowly gravitated to the areas best suited to their health. Those areas happened to be on a 50-foot sandstone terrace located between the rock garden and the lawn.

"First, drifts of my favorite wild red poppy appeared in two or three places, blooming more vigorously and colorfully than they had before. Next, portulaca—normally quite difficult to establish in beds—put in a surprise appearance on the sunniest part of the terrace. Then alyssum cascaded onto the sunny terrace," she said.

"By now the floral migration was on, and the penstemon, which had been unhappy in a well-tended bed, marched boldly out into the flat sandstone to flourish brilliantly. Evening primrose appeared, growing to fantastic proportions and far excelling anything found in its normal habitat, while another wild specimen—the little blue violet—became a permanent resident, cropping out between the cracks in blue masses.

"Since the development of the first terrace-dwellers far exceeded anything that had been planted in the nearby beds, I soon began to plan and regulate flower growth on the terrace, obtaining added beauty and color with practically no extra effort, and without interfering too much with what was going on. I also began to realize with increasing clarity the numerous advantages offered by the stone-mulched terrace and why my plants were seeking them out without being particularly invited or encouraged.

"Contrary to my expectations, the terrace newcomers did not wither for lack of moisture, nor was their growth stunted during the hot season. Because the porous sandstone seems to reduce evaporation, I found it necessary to water only when flower growth was dense and tall. Sometimes, when a stone broke or chipped, I lifted it to find the soil moist and pliant, well-aerated and teeming with active angleworms beneath. Capillary root growth became so pronounced that, in many instances, the tiny but vigorous root systems penetrated the stones themselves. Another growth-promoting factor came from the slow disintegration of the rocks which deposited rich minerals in the soil. In addition, most of the wild flowers prefer the slightly acid condition created by the sandstone," Mrs. Montfort said.

"Although I had long been aware of the many advantages of rock gardening, I now realized that a flat sandstone terrace offers the same benefits but on a much wider scale. Besides moisture storage and weed control, the stones moderate extremes of temperature, keeping the soil below them cool against the heat of the sun. Root growth is steady and vigorous, low foliage is protected against spattering when it rains, and a clean, attractive background is provided for creeping, low-lying blooms.

"It wasn't necessary to plant seeds deliberately on the terrace because other flower combinations occured quite spontaneously as highly welcome additions. Among these, the delphiniums established themselves in thick profusion—their curled green crowns appearing consistently between the cracks long before my regular beds even thawed.

"Such are the advantages of terrace gardening—however unintentional!—that early germination is now counted upon with confidence. Long before the frost was out of the ground in the garden, my poppies and portulaca put in a startlingly early appearance. Despite the freezing nights, cold winds and even intermittent snows, they continued to develop—hardy wild pioneers who know what's best for them and where to find it. Anyway, the snow melted quickly on the sunheated terrace before it could do any lasting harm.

"So," said Mrs. Montfort, "don't be dismayed if some of your favorite plants insist on wandering through your garden, away from the spots you have prepared so carefully and lovingly for them. They know what they're doing and what they're looking for, so don't fight 'em—encourage them. That's what I did, and the entire garden benefitted when my wild flowers insisted on moving over to my stone-mulched terrace."

Ruth Bixler's trees benefited when she turned to stone mulching. It was for her—like for the Woods—something of a last hope. After she and her husband acquired a small tract near Allentown, Pennsylvania, and constructed a home, she discovered their proposed garden plot was shale. A period of composting and mulching cured the gardening problems. But her flowers failed and her trees started to follow suit.

"When all my spruce trees died but one," she said, "I decided to do something about it. My fruit trees had a struggle to get rooted, too. A Chinese walnut tree gave up and died. I also realized then that the sprinkling system was not the answer.

"Why, I asked myself, does a tree grow high and handsome in the woods under the same sun, with no surplus water, and in my yard refuse to grow? Finally, I made a trip to the woods and the first thing I noticed was the stones under the trees. And then I knew that it was the stones that helped hold the moisture.

"In July of that year we spent our vacation along Lake Erie. The grade going down to the beach was full of round, flat stones. The day we started home, our car trunk was half full of these. That week I laid the last spruce thick with stone. In a month the tree started growing and stayed green all summer in spite of the hot, dry weather and few showers," she continued. "It never stopped growing and is now a beautiful specimen. The next year I brought more stones home and started putting them around the fruit trees. A Yellow Transparent apple tree grew quickly after the stones were put around, and has been bearing very heavily ever since."

Without realizing it, Mrs. Bixler may have been doing more for her trees than merely providing a handy reservoir. A. P. Thompson, a Shenandoah Valley orchardist, has been growing apples the organic way for years. Part and parcel of his method is mulching, with a generous number of stones included in the mulch. He cites not only the moisture conserving qualities of the stones as a reason, but others as well.

Thompson uses what he calls the "fortress method" of stone mulching, claiming it has four benefits. It gives the trees greater anchorage in strong winds. Further, it acts as a heat sink by absorbing a great deal of the sun's heat during the day. On frosty nights, this heat sets off minor convection currents that provide some protection to bud and bloom. The fortress also provides protection for the tree's roots from burrowing mice, which oftimes damage or kill trees. And finally, the rocks provide calcium and magnesium for the tree as they weather.

The fortress method, one of the most unusual of Thompson's many offbeat orchard management practices, involved erecting a six-inch high wall of half-inch dolomitic rock around the base of each tree. About 500 pounds of stone goes into each five or six foot diameter wall.

Servais, the Wisconsin rock collector, developed a similar technique for nurturing young trees. He explained his mulch, saying, "Last year I placed 100 pounds of rocks around two young pear trees and a blue plum as soon as I planted them, and then gave them a heavy soaking. I didn't want to lose them because of air pockets around their tender young roots—which has happened in the past.

"My trees all came through the summer in good, healthy condition, justifying my theory that the weight of the rocks gradually squeezes the air out of the newly worked, dampened soil," he said.

The experience of John S. MacManes with sick trees offers further evidence in support of J. I. Rodale's conclusion that rock mulches greatly benefit trees. Even the fertile ground of the Finger Lakes region of upstate New York couldn't do much for MacManes' sick peach tree.

"If we were going to save it all," MacManes decided, "we would have to rock-mulch it, we agreed, at the same time giving it plenty of compost, leaf mold and wood ashes in order to sustain its will to live. Otherwise, the tree looked bad on the following counts:

"1) It was too old, well past its prime;

"2) Leaf curl had blighted its foliage almost completely;

"3) It was suffering from gummosis, was ill-shaped and worm infested;

"4) The northwest wind hit it full blast throughout the winter.

" 'Cut it down,' the neighbors said, but we were stubborn. We had noted some timid and sparse new growth and felt that 'where there's life, there's hope.' So we pitched in, and I began my own private battle to save our tree," he continued.

"First I applied a booster dose of finely pulverized limestone right under the tree, and then added a generous top-dressing of good wood ashes. Next, starting at the drip line and working to within a few inches of the trunk, I heaped poultry droppings, leaf mold and compost. And finally, I worked over the entire area, setting a good ground cover of rock mulch to regulate soil temperature and moisture, to encourage extra bacterial growth in the soil, and also to supply the trace minerals which our tree obviously lacked. Then we sat back, eager with expectation, to see the results and reap our reward.

"Nothing happened. The tree didn't die and it didn't seem to be getting any better.

"But the spring and summer of the following year told a much different story, as the magic in stone mulching began to assert itself.

"The season came on extremely dry, which tended to slow up growth everywhere—what our tree needed was rain. But, despite the baking sun and drying winds, new growth took place before our eyes, and we were agreeably surprised and pleased with the richly vibrant bloom at blossom time. A beautiful green again enfolded our tree, leaf curl was reduced drastically, gummosis practically ceased.

"That harvest time we picked bushels of lusciously big peaches—each a handful in its own right—from our once-dying tree," he concluded.

Michigan planter Walter J. Muilenberg discovered that even the frail Canadian Hemlock tree can survive out of its element with a good rock mulch. In Muilenberg's area, the tree is never found in pure stands. It's always mixed in with hardwoods which protect it from wind and sun.

It seems impossible to transplant them and make them grow under ordinary conditions. Muilenberg was clearing land and pulling out stumps when he came upon three hemlocks. He decided to let them grow and cleaned out everything else around them. A lot of stones accumulated and by sheer accident they were piled under one of the hemlocks. That is the only one that lived. The other two died in a few years. The peculiar thing is that the one with the stone mulch became a wonderful specimen, far superior to the twisted and scraggly hemlocks usually seen in the forest.

"It is my guess that the third hemlock survived because of the rock, a weight of several tons, which had been piled around it," Muilenberg said. "It had grown up in heavy woods, which consequently helped to make it more shallow-rooted, and in heavy shade, which helped to keep the soil cool and moist. Later, when the rest of the trees were removed, rock gave the tree a good grip on the soil and made for a cool, moist root-run, as rock always does. It would seem that the top of the tree will get along in good shape so long as the roots have protection."

Stone mulches, of course, needn't be accidental, haphazard or last resorts. They can be tremendous additions to an existing garden or the center of a new one. A stone mulch can be exactly what you want it to be, because you can make the stones, as Robert Rodale once explained.

"My father, J. I. Rodale, has had the idea for many years that mulches don't have to be dull, and they don't have to be just organic either. Many a day in my youth was spent hauling rocks from quarry and fence row to make stone mulches for around trees, and even for lining the rows in a special vegetable garden. A stone mulch has certain advantages over any other kind. It lasts, for one thing. As the stone 'decays', it also adds minerals to the soil. But stone mulches have disadvantages, too. Their biggest problem is the odd sizes of stones, which make them difficult to fit together into a neat, flat surface. It can be done by an expert mason— but a person who isn't a mason might have trouble making a geometric pattern out of rock.

"The idea of making different-shaped concrete segments that would fit together into unusual stone mulches came to my father several years ago. He had some concrete molds made in square and rectangular shapes, and cast enough of the blocks to make several different beds. One of his concrete mulch variations is now an herb garden. The most-noticed one, though, is the round 'target' garden along the highway in front of my house.

"These concrete mulch gardens have turned out to be one of those unusual garden features which attract attention year after year. They are something you can make yourself, if you are handy with tools and can make the molds. The concrete work is simplicity itself, because no fine finishing is required. You can even make them in different colors by adding dye to the mix," he said.

The most commonly used shape in the Rodale garden is a triangle. In the mixture for the cement slabs are included some crushed rock and some mineral fertilizer powders like phosphate rock, granite dust and dolomite. These minerals slowly leach out into the soil. The recipe for the cement includes one part cement, one and a half part sand, one and a half part stone, a half part dolomite and a half part phosphate rock.

"We also add finely powdered coal dust to the mixture, not only for its minerals, especially sulphur, but also to darken the triangles, in order to make them retain heat better," J. I. explained.

"There are three different sizes of triangles, so that they can be made to fit together in a circular pattern. The sizes are 12 by 12 by 12 inches, 10 by 10 by 12 inches and 10 by 10 by 14 inches. The larger one is made with a pool-table billiard ball rack triangle. This was the idea of John Keck, our farmer-technician, who went at this project with great enthusiasm and who practically worked the whole thing out by himself. He made the slabs a few at a time, in his spare time, but it's surprising how little by little things add up.

"One of the advantages of this method is that once a year the slabs can easily be taken up and the soil given a complete working over," J.I. continued. "The most interesting thing about it is its beauty, and the fact that a person with some imagination can vary the designs. Almost any shape of metal form for the molds can be made by a welder or blacksmith."

"A lot of people get in a mulch rut," said the younger Rodale. "Perhaps they have one kind of mulch material available to them, and use it year after year. While that is the easy way, it can't be counted on to give the maximum in beauty to a garden. We should think more that the mulch around trees, shrubs and flowers is a dynamic feature of the garden, and not just something to hold down weeds, preserve moisture and feed the soil. Of course, those are the big reasons for mulching, but we shouldn't forget beauty as well.

"Mulches of small stones and gravel are becoming more popular lately, spurred perhaps by the Japanese school of landscape architecture which features such things as raked areas of sand and boulders artistically scattered throughout a garden," he said. "One of the most popular of these mulches is river gravel, the small stones collected from stream beds, where they have been washed and rolled by the waters for perhaps hundreds of years. Those stones all have rounded edges and are of a variety of colors. Best application for them is along a building or near areas of concrete such as walks or patios. They provide a welcome visual relief from flat, uninteresting pavement or big walls."

A stone mulch is, as Servais the rock collector said, adding "a bit of glamour" to your plants, "while helping them to grow better."

Chapter Six

WHY WE REJECT ONE of the MOST COMMON MULCHES

Extensive experimentation has shown marked increases in vegetable yields resulting from the use of black, polyethylene plastic mulches. Many gardeners have enthusiastically adopted the use of such mulches. It seems like such a good idea. But it's not.

Most people overlook one important fact. They see that plastic mulches are cheap, effectively control weeds and efficiently conserve moisture. And they fail to see that a plastic mulch contributes nothing to the fertility of the soil. It's only shelter, not food, too. An organic mulch is both.

When you stop to think about it, what could be more unnatural than a product like plastic mulch? Plastics are non-organic substances which add nothing to the soil except trouble if you try to grow crops where they have been buried. There is, in fact, some reason to believe that the formaldehyde given off in small amounts by some plastics can actually kill soil bacteria and thus interfere with plant growth.

The durability of plastic, at first counted as its prime virtue, has become instead a monumental pollution problem, for unless it is burned, plastic is virtually indestructible. Since burning certain kinds of plastic, particularly polyvinyl chloride, gives off toxic fumes such as hydrochloric acid—labeled by the New York City Commissioner of Air Resources as a "serious environmental hazard"—burning is not a safe disposal method. Even the DuPont Company, famed for creating "Better Living Through Chemistry," and a leading plastics manufacturer, has found no more satisfactory method of disposing of plastics than to bury them. Should we continue at our present pace, there will hardly be a square inch of land on the continent in which some form of plastic doesn't lurk six inches beneath the surface.

Studies into methods of degrading plastics have been conducted in the United States, Sweden, Great Britain and the Netherlands. No answer has been found, and many authorities are beginning to recognize that we are coming face to face with a very serious problem.

Ironically, organic gardeners, dedicated to preserving a healthful and attractive environment, are nevertheless unwittingly contributing their share to the nation's reputation as a plastic society. Without giving it a thought, most of us end up with at least half a dozen disposable but indestructible plastic packages every time we go to the supermarket. But more than that, some actually use plastics deliberately in their gardening!

Plastics are convenient, quick and durable. That they are a labor-saving mulch is plausible. After all, they don't have to be replaced periodically as do those organic mulches which keep disappearing into the soil. But the fact that the non-organic plastic mulch doesn't disappear—ever—is its prime drawback.

It should be noted that another increasingly popular non-organic mulch—if handled properly—doesn't have this drawback. That mulch is aluminum foil, which can be recycled. Aluminum foil mulch has many of the advantages of plastic mulch, plus some it doesn't have —such as an insect-repelling, photosynthesis-boosting reflectivity. But, like plastic, it won't ever boost the fertility or tone up the condition of your soil. If you must use a non-organic mulch, use aluminum foil. And when you're through with it, recycle it.

But before you do, read what Ruth Stout, that mulching pioneer, has to say about plastic mulches. Most of what she says will apply to aluminum foil mulches as well. Despite the plausibility of claims that plastic mulches cut the labor in mulch gardening, Miss Stout plans to stick with her tried and true methods.

"A month or so after my first book about year-round mulch was published in 1955, I got a letter from a business firm in New Jersey, asking permission to send me a gift of black plastic, which was, of course, to be used for mulching my garden," she said. "My reply was, in effect, as follows: 'Thank you very much for your offer, and since I never refuse a present, I will accept the plastic. However, I think it only fair to add that I may never use it. And if I do (just to try it out), I will almost certainly write about it and speak of it, not for it, but against it, comparing it unfavorably with the kind of mulch I use.'

"Needless to say, that New Jersey firm didn't send me any plastic.

"In writing about gardening, and giving talks on the subject, I try very hard to stick to my own experiences. However, all one needs, in my opinion, in order to be able to figure out what's wrong with plastic mulching is a little imagination and a little common sense.

"Let's say that a person who was rather short-changed when imagination was being passed around decides to use a plastic mulch instead of hay on a garden the size of mine (45 x 50); he figures that, for one thing, the plastic will cost less, since it lasts forever. Well, here's news for him. Plastic won't be cheaper because, since it doesn't supply the nourishment needed to keep a garden producing, he will also have to buy fertilizer each year to make sure that his plants get what a mulch of hay gives them; the hay rots and provides the soil with all the required nutrients" she continued.

"And of course all other vegetable and organic matter that rots—straw, leaves, corncobs, wood chips, kitchen garbage—will nourish your soil; cornstalks and the tomato, bean, asparagus plants should all be left on your plot, in order to do their share of providing nutrients.

"I have heard it said that there is less to do in a garden if you use a plastic mulch rather than an organic one, and I wonder how growers operate when using the former. Since it seems to be less work, I suppose they just spread the plastic on their plot in strips, then ignore the whole thing.

"For the moment I am going to pretend that for some odd reason I've decided to use plastic for mulch on my 45-by-50 plot. Let's say that I put down strips of plastic, leaving a small space between, and I drop the seeds in the exposed area. But first I must do something about enriching the soil, and maybe buy some organic fertilizer. But what? Manure? And do I make a compost pile? I'll certainly skip that, for it's quite a lot of work to get the materials together. Then, when the pile has become rich soil, I'd have to load a wheelbarrow with it and distribute it all around. Well, that whole routine is 'out of bounds' as far as I'm concerned," she continued.

"Now I go ahead and put in the seeds in my plastic-mulched garden and the plants show up and so do the weeds—in the spaces between the plants right in the rows which have to be made rather far apart. That is, the corn does, and potatoes, and squash, and tomatoes and, in fact, almost all the plantings. The question of weeds isn't a problem, of course, if you use an organic mulch. The hay, or whatever you use, is lying there in the row, as well as alongside it, and will keep just about all weeds from getting anywhere.

"At last, the first summer of plastic-mulching my plot is over, and finally another spring shows up—time to plant early crops. But when I go out to the garden, I'm nonplussed; I can't get rid of the idea that the plastic which was supposed to save me a lot of work, should certainly be moved to other areas. Why do I feel that? Well, I keep thinking of that good earth under the plastic, and it seems absurd not to make any use of it. And the small open space, which I used for planting last season, doesn't seem to be adequate now, so the only thing to do is to move those black strips to other spots, and that would certainly be a tedious job. (I will admit that maybe I am being unreasonable, and that it may be quite all right to cover up a lot of your soil with plastic and never produce anything in those areas, but the whole idea sounds goofy to me.)

"However, if a person is wise enough to use organic matter for mulch, all he has to do in early spring if he wants to plant some lettuce and parsley in whatever spot he may choose, is just pull the hay aside (if he hasn't already done that in the fall) and put in the seeds.

"About asparagus, I just can't believe that anyone at all familiar with how this vegetable operates would use plastic in that bed. Asparagus likes to wander around and come up wherever it pleases. And it likes a rich soil —just as weeds do, unfortunately. But an organic mulch will, as I said, dispose almost entirely of the latter. As you may know, asparagus stalks can, and will, push up through a hay mulch, which they could of course never be able to do if your plot is mulched with plastic.

"You also may know that air, rain, dew and sun reach the soil right through organic mulch. A plastic covering keeps all of these beneficial things from reaching the earth, although it's true that plastic will keep the ground damper than it would be if the soil stayed bare. But hay and leaves not only keep the earth moist, but also let dew and rain enter the soil, and help to hold the moisture in.

"Since I started to use organic mulch, we have had several seasons with long droughts—one summer no rain at all for three consecutive months. Although I can't water any plants in dry weather because my well is very shallow, yet I didn't lose one vegetable through those dry spells. Squash needs lots of water but despite that season with a three-months drought, I had an over-supply—one of the Blue Hubbards weighed 51 pounds," she said.

"When óne of my neighbors (a confirmed organic gardener and mulcher) dropped in, I spoke of this plastic. Although I knew she didn't use it, I asked her if she could think of anything at all in favor of it as a mulch.

"My neighbor said that plastic is supposed to warm up the soil more quickly than hay. When I asked why she thought this, she hesitated for a moment then said that someone must have told her it did. 'Well, even if it does, what's so important about that?' I asked. 'You can, for instance, plant lettuce on frozen ground, and it doesn't seem to mind. After all, it's only early plantings that need warmed-up soil; the sun does the job for later crops. So for parsley, lettuce, peas, all you need do is take the hay off those areas in the fall and, in my experience, the ground is then never too cold to interfere with desired results.'

"She had one more suggestion which she thought might be favorable, and that was that since squash plants take up so much room in a garden, black plastic might make it easier to keep down weeds between the hills. However, I plant squash between my two rows of asparagus, and I've already said why I wouldn't use plastic for the latter, even if I went a little haywire and wanted to do so," she concluded.

If you are concerned about producing those abundant, nutritional crops next year and next decade and next generation, you, like Ruth Stout, won't mulch with plastic. You'll find it cheaper to spend once—if at all—for a good organic mulch which will rot and fertilize your soil in time. You'll find you can do as well or better without plastic, the indestructible, non-nutritional mulch.

.... AN ALTERNATIVE TO PLASTIC MULCH

So now the whole mulch idea has been ruined for you. Plastic mulch was all you were looking for in a mulch. Using it, you didn't have to scour the world for lumberyards with excess sawdust or farmers with spoiled hay or harrass your neighbors for leaves and grass clippings —they were beginning to think you daft, right?—or even continually spend money for more, since that organic stuff *did* keep disappearing. You could be completely respectable and order some from your local plastic mulch store, put it down in the garden and forget it. Well, maybe those shiny black indestructible strips in your garden lacked the visual appeal of a variety of rocks mulching away, or the warm richness of a layer of cocoa bean shells, some other natural mulch. But it could be acquired without people giving you funny looks and it didn't mess up the inside of the car and . . .

But it's ruined, right? Okay, try this. Use newspapers.

After you've read all the news, go out and throw it on the ground. It's one of the most effective ground coverings around. And it's organic. Even the ink provides trace elements vital to healthy plant life. Chances are, you have stacks of newspapers in your basement, just sitting there gathering dust and creating a fire hazard when they could be in the garden decomposing busily and creating good, rich soil.

Environmentally-minded mulchers have found that mulching with newspapers not only provides a great way to safely recycle as much as 50 per cent of our refuse but also to control weeds, improve soil texture and regulate moisture and temperature in the garden. They have been using newspapers for years to create a humus which is readily incorporated into the soil.

Here are some of the ways they've been doing it.

1) Laying them out in varying thicknesses of unfolded sheets, leaving space for rows or planting in holes punched through the paper;

2) Shredding or tearing the sheets into a fine aggregate which can be easily handled in beds and borders, also around trees and shrubs;

3) Using them as a liner under materials to conserve moisture;

4) Burying them with the family garbage in selected areas after tearing them into very small fragments;

5) Converting them into a highly mobile, flowing slurry by combining them with water in a pulping machine.

Mrs. Sherrelle Ault slides unfolded newspapers under "poultry netting" one foot wide. Number 9 wire or coat-hanger wire cut about eight inches long, is bent into a "U" which goes on each side about three feet apart, and is pushed into the soil.

Newspapers eight layers thick keep trees and shrubs free from weeds.

"To renew the newspapers each year—and you must as they decompose underneath," the Missourian said, "take out the wire U's on one side, slide fresh newspapers under the wire, and replace the U's. I don't try to do the whole garden at once, but just go along—150 feet of wire costs $5 here. But I don't need to buy it again because it lasts and lasts.

"The appearance is fine," she said. She also explained how she used newspaper and waste pulp to tame her stubborn hardpan garden soil.

"I have gumbo cement for a garden, and lots of luck to anyone who tries to plow on that site—no telling what else was buried there by a bulldozer. This was the only way to go ahead. Not being able to dig down deeper than one inch, and being on low ground which stands in water, the only thing to do was to build on top.

"This is also a great way to dispose of all your paper trash. Fold everything to about the size of a folded newspaper. This goes for cereal boxes and containers of all sizes (tear them open), wrappings—everything—because the wire holds them down and keeps them from blowing all over the landscape. Paper egg cartons—practically wood pulp—should be torn up and worked into the soil."

"I hope that mulching your garden with newspapers will be a continuing and growing movement," said Mrs. Margaret Hunter of Lake Worth, Florida. "I have been doing it for years, with more than one good result, the re-use of newspapers," she continued. She asserted that, "newspapers control some of the garden pests.

"I tried it with very good results on some pests including white fly, some scales and aphids. At first I just put down three-or-four-inch-thick piles of folded papers, held down with just a piece of wood or rock around shrubs. With time, I began tearing the paper into strips, and covering the ground with them which permitted more uniform watering from the hose or the rain. I also found that the torn strips stayed put better and didn't blow around.

"As horticulture chairman of the garden club, I talked about the advantages of paper mulch to the members. After they came and saw my torn paper borders, many of them followed my example and I later received reports that they had obtained good results from using newspaper as a mulch."

Newspapers, dampened and torn into 30-inch long strips, will "tangle good when stirred lightly," Mrs. Hunter said. Method of dampening is not important just as long as the paper "flutters down in limp strips and no longer clings together in clumps.

"My garden is quite small," she reported. "I put the paper around the 'up' squash hills and along the newly planted okra row. When the okra was up and large enough to thin, I pulled the paper together with the plants. Considering the poor soil in this place, the okra is doing quite well as are most of the other vegetables and herbs. I am building up a good organic soil and the paper mulch is proving a big help."

Robert F. DeVoe, Sr., has followed organic gardening methods in eight different homesteads since he got started back in 1923. Today, he lives in Meadowvale, "a small town east of Louisville, Kentucky," where he mulches his vegetable garden and his strawberries with newspapers.

"I spread newspapers three to six thicknesses with

three-inch overlaps on all four sides over my vegetable garden," he said. "I covered this with the mulch pile which consisted of kitchen refuse, wood bark, weeds, grass clippings, flower and bush trimmings and cotton-seed meal. I wet this down for several days before planting.

"I started with a few bush beans, and corn in peat pots, and placed them in rows. But at the east end I dug holes in the mulch and newspaper and placed the plants and seeds in the soil. Along the fence, I set out strawberry plants in newspapers with grass clippings on top and brick edging to make everything look neat and keep the papers from blowing."

Still another newspaper mulcher is Paul Graybill, who gathers grass cuttings, wood chips, fallen leaves, hay, weeds and vegetable refuse—garbage included—and then returns them to the soil together with a paper mulch.

"Without all the nutrients that organic materials add to the soil, my fruit and vegetables would have very little taste and practically no food value," said the Connecticut homesteader.

The surface mulching Graybill worked out overcomes many problems he's encountered in other methods. When plants reach a height of two or three inches and the ground is thoroughly warmed, he scatters fine organic material such as heap-prepared compost, grass clippings, shredded leaves or fine hay between the rows.

Next, he folds newspapers about four papers thick, places them in the rows and between or against the plants on each side, then scatters an inch or so of grass clippings, hay or other organic material on top to hold them in place. This type of mulch lasts through the season—without further work. Additional fine material may be added during the growing period. Very few weeds come up, Graybill said, except a few now and then directly in the plant row, which can be easily pulled because the soil stays so moist and friable. Another advantage: the fruit and leaves of plants are kept clean, and the compost below the papers disintegrates fast. The paper itself decomposes by fall, ahead of preparations for the cover crop seeding.

When setting out young plants like tomatoes and cabbage, Graybill tears a slot in the paper, making it fit snugly around the stem, then covers the entire area about the plant before adding compost over the paper. He says he likes the paper-mulched method much better than plastic sheets, since it allows free moisture passage during rains and also allows some "breathing", where plastic—unless perforated—allows no passage of water or air.

The paper-mulch plan is effective in the strawberry patch, Graybill said. Runners can be controlled by placing folded papers of 10 or more thicknesses between the rows in spring and covering this with hay. This leaves exposed a bed of strawberries about eight inches to a foot wide in the row itself. And it kills the runners which are covered, holds moisture, and keeps the strawberries clean during the bearing season. He thins these narrow beds by pulling out plants after picking season.

Newspaper mulching works two-fold wonders. It is a good organic mulch in the garden. It relieves the community of a portion of its increasingly heavy burden of solid waste. So send that plastic back to its maker and mulch instead with newspapers.

Chapter Seven

THERE'S METHOD
in THIS MULCHING

Hopefully, you've been convinced. And you've run out and gathered up all the mulching materials you could lay your hands on. Now you're standing beside the garden, hay in hand, with a slightly quizzical expression. There're a couple of questions. . . . . .

"When do I mulch? How much do I use? How often should I mulch?" you're asking. "What about fertilizers? Don't I need fertilizers at all? Are you sure this is as easy as it sounds? I'm going to goof it up, right? Because there's something you forgot to tell me, right?"

Just relax. Mulching is as easy as it sounds. You won't goof it up as long as you are careful and follow a few guidelines. We won't give you the steps of the perfect way to mulch your garden, because such a way doesn't exist. We will point out mulching guidelines and a few of the most common pitfalls. A good organic

115

gardener, of course, always likes to experiment a bit and develop a specially-adapted method. Thus the variations on when and how to mulch are as numerous as the materials you can use. We'll give you the maps. You'll have to select your own route.

The answer that Ruth Stout always gives to the first question—when should the mulching begin?—is "NOW, whatever the date may be." That's as good an answer as you can expect. There are, basically, three kinds of mulching—summer, winter and continuous. Miss Stout is of the continuous school of mulching. Other experienced mulchers find fault with a continuous covering and opt for covering their garden soil only a part of the year.

The chief reason for a mulch in winter is to prevent damage to plants from alternate freezing and thawing which causes soil to heave and expose and break roots. Winter mulches, too, protect the more tender plants not perfectly suited to rougher climates. And they protect plants against rapid changes of temperature. In many sections the temperature often ranges from 15 to 20 degrees in 24 hours. Under a mulch the temperature remains more constant.

The mulch should be applied *after* the first hard frost to prevent alternate thaws and freezes from heaving soil, roots or bulbs. Its purpose once winter sets in is to hold the lower temperature *in* the soil, avoiding thaw and subsequent refreezing which shifts the earth and plants, often exposing enough roots to cause winter-killing. To protect young shrubs, and particularly roses, mound several inches of earth around them early in autumn, then mulch after the first freeze with several more inches of leaves, straw, yard trimmings, or other mulch materials.

The winter carpet of organic matter also helps condition the whole garden area for the next spring.

A summer mulch, applied as soon as plants are established, allows the temperature under it to rise and fall gradually, to remain uniform and about 10 to 15 degrees cooler than that of unmulched areas close by during normal air temperatures.

The more even, cooler temperature under a mulch helps to maintain a better balance between the plant's loss of water (transpiration) and its absorption of water. It does this even during hot, dry days when transpiration exceeds absorption and causes unmulched plants to wilt. A mulch acts as a reservoir. It conserves water by providing a greater area for absorption and an uneven textured surface which prevents water from running off.

After you've planted most of your vegetables your primary concern will be how to protect these plants from the coming summer's hot, dry weather. What should you do? Mulch.

The third kind of mulch, the continuous mulch, serves the dual purpose of both the summer and winter mulch. It protects whatever plants are in the ground and steadily works to condition the soil. A mulch used the year around serves to control weeds, conserve moisture and provide plants with protection against the extremes of weather. If it is one of the coarse materials with rough, irritating surfaces, it will discourage slugs and snails from crawling over plants and damaging them.

A continuous mulch around thick-stemmed perennials, shrubs, trees, evergreens should be of a coarse, heavy material not subject to rapid decay. Straw, hay or cotton bolls may not appeal to you for this purpose because they break down fast and must be replenished regularly.

Woody materials and coarsely ground cobs are ideal. They last from three to five years, when applied to a depth of three to four inches, and relieve the gardener of the chore of cultivation and worries concerning drought and heaving of soil. The only maintainenance such mulches need is a nitrogenous fertilizer in spring and midsummer and a raking, when necessary, to open them up to air and water.

Most of the hard-core mulchers—like those whose experiences with mulching have been related—use a continuous mulch. But they generally have some reservations about the continuousness of the cover.

There *can* be too much of a good thing. There can be advantages to pulling back the mulch on certain occasions to allow the ground to warm. And while a year-round mulch does the job on sandy soil, it can defeat the purpose on heavy clay.

Most gardeners agree that mulch timing is important to produce bumper crops and have learned by their own mistakes or experiences to abide by a few general rules.

Seedlings planted in very moist soil should not be mulched immediately. The addition of any organic matter which keeps the soil at a high humidity encourages damping-off of young plants. Damping-off is a disease caused by a fungus inhabiting moist, poorly ventilated soil, and can be 90 per cent fatal. Allow seedlings to become established then, before mulching.

It is wise, too, to consider the danger of crown-rot in perennials. This disease is also caused by a fungus. If there have been especially heavy rains, postpone mulching until the soil is no longer water-logged. Do not allow mulches composed of peat moss, manure, compost, or ground corn cobs to touch the base of these plants. Leave a circle several inches in diameter. The idea here is to permit the soil to remain dry and open to the air around the immediate area of the plant.

Do not mulch a wet, low-lying soil, or at most, use only a dry, light type of material, such as salt hay or buckwheat hulls. Leaves are definitely to be avoided as they may mat down and add to the sogginess.

The heavy mulching method described by Ruth Stout stands a better chance of success if the soil contains some humus (well-decayed organic matter) and is fairly high in nitrogen content.

Where the soil is poor and mostly clay in composition, it is well to test the soil and apply the needed elements, as nitrogen, phosphate and potash, according to test results. Then spread the mulch in thin layers without packing, so as to permit air and moisture to start breaking down the raw materials. When the first layer of mulch shows signs of decay, sprinkle some cottonseed meal, blood meal or other nitrogen-rich material and apply another thin layer of mulch. By this method, any danger of the heavy mulch taking too much nitrogen from the soil is avoided.

Some vegetables, like tomatoes and corn, need a thoroughly warmed soil to encourage ideal growth. A mulch applied too early in the spring, before ground temperatures have had a chance to climb a little in frost-zone areas, may slow up such crops. Once plants are well started, though, and the weather levels off, mulch is definitely in order to conserve needed water, stimulate topsoil microorganisms and generally condition the soil.

Author-gardener John Krill pinpointed the importance of logical mulch timing for tomatoes, for example. His experiments—and the experiences of others—show that early ripening of tomatoes cannot be expected if the spring-thawing ground is cloaked too soon.

"Mulch can be a hindrance instead of a benefit under certain conditions. The deeper the mulch, the greater the drawback," he said. "I'm a mulch addict for more years than I care to name. If I named how many people would say 'He's too old to know better'. Yet I will venture that many mulch enthusiasts have undergone the same experiences I have.

"With the coming of the true spring weather, I'd be in the garden planting tomatoes. The plants were set properly and lovingly in their holes. Then I'd carefully mulch them with any suitable substance available," he said. "The plants never failed to respond and grow sturdily. Their color was a green to delight the eye of the most critical gardener. As the mulch would compact itself, I would busily add more. There wasn't a weed to be found because the mulch prevented them from coming up.

"Ah! That part of growing tomatoes was simply unbeatable. But guess who had the first *ripe* tomatoes? None other than the people across the street. They didn't mulch because they had not yet learned of its tremendous value. They weren't the only ones. Friends living miles away and scattered in every direction also had ripe tomatoes sooner than I.

"What hurt me the worst was that I had given tomato plants to them from my hotbeds. Why did their tomatoes ripen ahead of mine since they were of the same identical stock? Sure, I couldn't help noting that their unmulched plants did not produce as much. Nor did they last until frost finally destroyed them, as was the case with my own mulched plants. Hot and dry weather withered and destroyed their plants long before a frost came, while mine were just coming into heavy production of ripe fruit.

"There had to be a connection between mulched and non-mulched plants. A little serious thinking prompted me to conduct a simple, but extremely illuminating experiment. When spring once more arrived, I had my experiment ready to try. I set out three rows of tomatoes. All the plants came from the same hot-bed. The first row I covered with mulch as I had always done. I left the second row bare. No mulch was applied. And during the growing season I kept this row well cultivated. I did not water these unmulched plants because I had never watered those I did mulch. The only thing I did was keep the soil loose and weed-free. It turned out that it was a season of ample rains and watering would have been totally unnecessary. The natural moisture was a definite help in the experiment.

"The third row was also left unmulched—up to a point. As soon as the tomato blossoms appeared, I gave up clean cultivation of this row and covered it with a straw mulch. The other row which I had left clean and without mulch also showed a good set of blossom. But the mulched row was just showing signs of developing buds. It would take 10 to 15 days to produce the blossoms that were already in bloom on the two unmulched rows.

"The mystery was clearing up. Sure enough, the unmulched row produced the first ripe fruit. Almost neck-and-neck with it ripened the fruit in the row I had mulched after flowers had appeared. The fruit was heavier, juicier and far better shaped than in the row which had been left unmulched. The mulched row? It was the same old story. The plants were beautifully

Mulching of tomato plants too early in the season can slow ripening.

green and just loaded with fine-shaped green tomatoes. There wasn't a single ripe tomato among them. It would be two weeks or more before there would be any ripe ones," he said.

"But I had the key to the whole thing. By mulching the tomatoes when I had set them out in the spring, I had slowed down their growth. It takes a lot of heat to warm the soil in the spring to where it will stay warm. The mulch I had applied so soon had simply insulated the soil against absorbing warmth from the sun and air. Tomatoes like plenty of warmth. With the mulch keeping the soil from warming thoroughly, the plants were late in setting their blossoms. Consequently the fruit developed and ripened tardily. That this was so was easily proved. I laid my hand on the bare ground. It felt warm. I thrust my hand under the mulch. The sensation was one of soft coolness, something that the plants would tolerate, but which would not accelerate rapid development.

"How about the row I had mulched after the blossoms appeared? It was a dandy. By the time the flowers had developed, the soil was thoroughly warmed by the advancing heat of summer. The thin mulch now acted to prevent the warmth from leaving if sudden cool days and nights arrived. With heat under the mulch and more heat beaming on top of the mulch, these plants set heavy and well-shaped fruit that ripened practically as soon as that of the unmulched row," he said.

"About the middle of August the unmulched row began to shrivel and dry from a prolonged spell of heat and drought. The plants soon died. But the remaining two rows with their mulch coverings seemed to wax even more vigorously, with the row that had been mulched from the very start now coming into full ripening. Both of these rows produced good tomatoes until frost.

"I have learned this lesson: that if mulch is applied before the earth is thoroughly warmed, it will delay the ripening of tomatoes. I apply mulch now only when flowers are profuse, or even wait until the fruit sets before mulching the plants. Then the mulch seals the heat in instead of sealing it out. Thus it pays to know when to mulch.

"For late-ripening tomatoes I mulch my plants heavily when I set them out. For the earliest possible I set out enough to get ripe fruit in unmulched soil until the juicier and better-flavored tomatoes are ripened in the mulched rows. By the wise use of mulch you can prevent tomatoes ripening all at one time.

Bart Burdick confirmed Krill's conclusion.

"My garden was located approximately four miles south of Cornucopia, Wisconsin, which is Wisconsin's northernmost village," he said. "Temperatures drop to 20 to 30 degrees below zero—and occasionally to 40 below in midwinter. In spring the ground is slow to warm up.

"I set out my tomato plants in peat pots. My brother-in-law set out his plants a week later, minus peat pots. I mulched mine; he didn't. His tomatoes ripened seven to 10 days before mine. His ran out faster due to frost. Mine kept ripening for another week," Burdick explained.

"My conclusion as to the difference in time of

maturity: the same as John Krill. I should have left the mulch off *until* the soil had warmed sufficiently, then applied my mulch" he said.

In North Carolina Vernon Ward plowed and harrowed, then mulched the ground with about six to eight inches of wheat straw. Then, using Rutgers plants, he set his tomato plants through the mulch at a distance of four feet apart each way. To set the plants he pulled the mulch apart and set the roots in the prepared ground, then pushed the mulch back together around the stems. This was the end of his work. He did nothing else the entire season but pick tomatoes. Dark green vines soon completely covered and obliterated the mulch. No weeds grew. There was an immense set of fine tomatoes which remained large, with hardly any culls throughout the growing season, and the vines were still full of tomatoes at frost.

Ruth Stout mulches continuously and heavily. Unlike some gardeners, she doesn't differentiate between summer and winter mulches. She doesn't plow under the winter covering in spring, although many gardeners do this successfully. She doesn't plow at all. She is a strong believer in the continuous mulch, but she doesn't quarrel with the likes of John Krill and even admits to pulling back the mulch from ground slated to receive certain plants—like tomatoes—in spring. She has advice on the best ways to use mulches around your plants at spring planting time.

For spinach, lettuce and peas you should place six to eight inches of mulch. Shade the lettuce if you can. For beets, carrots, parsnips and kohlrabi: first thin the plants; then water thoroughly and put mulch all around them at once, six inches deep between rows. If the mulch is wet, so much the better. For bush beans: if already planted, thin, water and mulch. If you haven't planted them already, make a drill four inches deep; plant the beans sparsely; cover with two inches of soil; water; cover with a board or cardboard and mulch. Remove the board as soon as beans sprout. For corn: if planted already, thin to two plants in a hill instead of customary three. Water and put down six inches of mulch. (If you're running out of mulch, use as many layers of wet cardboard as you can collect. The cardboard is only an emergency measure; it is not as satisfactory as hay or leaves, because the latter provide more valuable nutrients to the soil as they decompose.) Each time you plant corn soak the seed overnight, make four-inch drills and cover the seed with two inches of soil. Water thoroughly, put a board over the seed and mulch immediately.

For late cabbage, broccoli, cauliflower, peppers, and tomatoes: if not planted yet, put very deep and four feet apart, mulching heavily. If peppers and tomatoes aren't in, put them very deep and farther apart than customary. If already planted, water and mulch heavily (six to eight inches).

For flowers: "All flower beds should be under a constant mulch, drought or no drought." Miss Stout said that you can easily do this without making them look ugly. Peonies can be mulched with dead leaves and their own tops. Well-rotted hay, mixed with crushed leaves, makes an excellent cover for roses. Put it on six inches deep and then scatter soil on top. It all looks like soil then, but the mulch is so deep that weeds can't sprout. The same method works well for large annuals, such as zinnias.

For small, low-growing annuals, Miss Stout used a fine mulch. "Since I keep my whole vegetable garden mulched constantly, there is always material there, not quite rotted enough to be rich soil, but rotted enough to look like it. I put this round my small annuals. If you don't have such material, you can use crushed leaves mixed with a little soil and wood ashes. This may sound like quite a job, but you have to do it just once a season."

The catch in mulching—if really there is one—lies in deciding on the amount of mulch to use. Should a good mulch always be the same depth? Must it be measured to slide-rule accuracy to function right? Do any other considerations influence the proper quantity? In other words, how much mulch is enough?

Generally, gardeners mulch crops that are in the garden for most of the summer. How much? During the growing season, the thickness of the mulch should be sufficient to prevent the growth of weeds. A thin layer of finely shredded plant materials is more effective than unshredded loose material. For example, a four to six-inch layer of sawdust will hold down weeds as well as eight or more inches of hay, straw or a similar loose, "open" material. So will one or two inches of buckwheat or cocoa bean hulls, or a two-to-four inch depth of pine needles. Leaves and corn stalks should be shredded or mixed with a light material like straw to prevent packing into a soggy mass. In a mixture, unshredded leaves can be spread eight to 12 inches deep for the winter. To offset the nitrogen shortage in sawdust and other low-nitrogen materials, add some compost, soybean or cottonseed meal.

Ground corncobs are highly recommended. Light and bulky, they help to "fluff up" the soil, thus preventing crust formation. Peat moss, an old stand-by, can be spread an inch or more in vegetable gardens and flower beds or used as a half-inch top-dressing twice a year on established lawns. Other good materials which can be used in the same manner include cotton gin wastes shredded cotton burrs, oat, rice and cottonseed shells and sphagnum moss.

How much mulch do you need? For her system of year-round mulching, Miss Stout says, you should put down, "more than you would think. You should start with a good eight inches of it. Then I'm asked: 'How can tiny plants survive between eight-inch walls?' And the answer to that is: the mulch is trampled on, rained on and packed down by the time you are ready to plant. It doesn't stay eight inches high."

Once you've put the basic mulch down, it is going to start decomposing and it will need replenishing periodically. How often do you replenish? That's something you will have to determine by observing the breakdown and compaction of your mulch. According to Miss Stout, the time to add to the cover is "whenever you see a spot that needs it. If weeds begin to peep through, don't bother to pull them; just toss an armful of hay on them."

Speaking simply, the amount of mulch to use is the amount that does the best job for you, your soil and your plants. Working out an ideal mulch program takes some experimenting, some trials with various materials and depths. It's only common sense to check on the most plentiful free and reasonable sources, to test the effects of different mulches in your climate locale, your own soil type and timing.

Are mistakes ever made in mulching? Of course. But with simple precautions you can avoid them. Before tossing armfuls of hay around, remember to use a partly rotted mulching material. New mulch will sometimes rob the soil of nitrogen. If you have only a small amount of decomposed material, put just a thin layer of it on the ground, then sprinkle some nitrogen-rich fertilizer such as bone meal, manure, cottonseed meal or tankage on the topsoil first. Another important thing is that mulch will be more effective if put on after a good rain—for it is difficult for water to penetrate a thick covering. If the ground is dry to start with, it will stay dry the rest of the summer unless the skies really open up.

"As wonderful as mulching is, it must be done right or the results may be disappointing," said Lucille Shade. "During my first few years I made many mistakes. For instance, I mulched corn with bright new hay and wondered why it didn't do well—without realizing that this brought a temporary nitrogen shortage as the hay started to decompose. I mulched other crops with oat straw and got a fine but unwanted crop of green oats between the rows of vegetables. I used timothy hay as a winter mulch for strawberries—and the following spring I had timothy coming up all over the strawberry bed. Nothing is harder to discourage when it's up close around the plants. I finally gave up and started a new strawberry patch," explained the Ohioan.

"Over the years I've learned some techniques that

make for successful mulching every time.

"First, if it is at all possible, use partly rotted mulching material. New mulch will rob your soil of nitrogen, which explains why my corn did so poorly under a mulch the first time I tried it. If you have only a small amount of partly decomposed material, put just a thin layer of it on the ground, then cover it with a thick layer of new stuff. If you must use all new mulch, then sprinkle some nitrogen-rich fertilizer such as blood meal, manure, cottonseed meal or tankage on the topsoil first. The only place I use new mulch without extra nitrogen is in covering large areas of ground—such as in the melon, cucumber and tomato patches—with rotted mulch up close around the plants.

"To age baled hay or straw in a hurry, soak it thoroughly with water, then give it six to eight weeks to start decaying," she said.

"A second important thing I've learned is that mulch will be much more effective if I wait until we've had a good rain, and then put it on—for it is difficult for water to penetrate a thick covering. If the ground is dry to start with, it will stay dry the rest of the summer unless the skies really open up. My spring gardening season is divided into dry and wet days. On wet days I concentrate on mulching, leaving all other chores for dry days.

"I've also discovered that simply pulling the mulch apart in the spring and planting my seed doesn't work on my heavy clay soil. I must open up a space about a foot wide in order to let the sun warm up the soil. I'm especially careful not to hurry mulching of such warm-weather lovers as tomatoes and melons. I start at the outer edges of my melon patch, for instance, and keep covering the ground until I get within about a foot of the vines. Then—once the weather is good and warm and the melons are off to a good start—I finish the job, mulching in close around the vines. In my climate, I've

Best time to mulch is after a shower. Small weeds are smothered out with hay.

found it's best to hold off close-up mulching of tomatoes until they have started to set fruit," she said.

"If your mulch starts sprouting—as my oat straw did —simply turn it over. It takes only a few minutes to walk down a row flipping it upside down.

"I am more careful now in selecting hay for a winter covering on strawberries. The trick is to use hay that was cut early, before the timothy became ripe enough to shed its seed. You can do this by opening up a bale and shaking it. If fine, chaff-like seed falls out, don't use it for this purpose.

"Nothing you can do to your garden will benefit it more than mulching," Mrs. Shade concluded. "It can substitute for the chemical gardener's watering, fertilizing, soil conditioning, and hours of weeding. What else can do so much for you?"

Morton Binder ran into nitrogen problems similar to those of Mrs. Shade. Binder, you may recall, turned to a mulching program to solve his soil problems. While still in the soil conditioning stage of his program, Binder wanted to set out some canned fuchsia without waiting.

"I dug the holes," he said, "and added two shovels of leaf mold from the woods to the sawdust soil mixture. As soon as the fuschias were set out, I mulched them with manure to begin to offset the lack of available nitrogen during the rotting-down process of the sawdust. The results were as follows—and, I think the moral of the story and the lessons learned may prove valuable to others attempting the same trick:

"In spite of the manure, the fuchsias rather quickly developed nitrogen starvation symptoms. I gave them a handful of processed sewage and a tablespoon of blood meal, but it wasn't until three months had elapsed that the color returned and the results became satisfactory.

"The other portion of the bed was not planted until four months after the first. These plants developed no chlorosis, and normal feeding brought out good color. Four months later both groups of plants appeared quite healthy, and no different in final results," Binder said.

"It proves again what has often been said. 'Don't plant immediately in freshly prepared soil where unrotted organic material has been used in large quantities. Wait until the breakdown process has had time to work.'"

The reason for these gardeners' woes is that substantial amounts of nitrogen are required for decomposing plant residues. When an organic mulching material does not contain all the nitrogen required for decomposition, the mulch tends to "borrow" nitrogen from the soil or fertilizer applied to the soil, leaving less nitrogen available for plant growth during the decomposition process. Consequently, signs of nitrogen deficiency are frequently observed in plants grown under heavy mulches, unless sufficient nitrogen fertilizer is added to compensate for the soil or fertilizer nitrogen required in the decomposition process. The amount of additional nitrogen fertilizer needed to compensate for the nitrogen tieup varies with the type of mulch and its state of decomposition.

Duration and severity of the nitrogen depression sometimes observed following application of organic mulches is affected by a number of factors in addition to the kind of mulching material used and its nitrogen content. Soil fertility—particularly the amount of nitrogen in the soil—is a significant factor in determining whether or not crop yields will be affected adversely under mulching. This is illustrated by studies of wheat grown in various sections of the west. Although yields grown under a system of mulch farming tended to be less than under moldboard plowing in most areas studied, no depressing effect on grain yields was observed in areas where the nitrate content of the soil was high.

Increases in the amount of soil nitrate following application of mulch occur under some conditions. In fact, such an increase has been reported in the majority of studies in which "inert" mulches such as plastic were used.

When decomposable mulches such as straw or hay or manure are used, the rate of decomposition and the proportion of carbon to nitrogen are significant factors in determining whether mulching will increase or decrease the nitrate content of the soil.

The point is that mulched crops must have an abundant nitrogen fertilizer supply, else the crop will show temporary nitrogen starvation. This is true because soil bacteria stimulated by the better growth conditions under the mulch tend to gobble up available soil nitrogen. Of course, these tiny motes of vegetable life soon die and decay, and give back to the soil quickly available higher-plant food. But there is a lag when you first mulch during which they need to be fed extra nitrogen.

This is why experienced mulchers like Ruth Stout sprinkle a bit of cottonseed meal or blood meal on the soil before planting. The soil can be treated with compost or manure, but Miss Stout doesn't go in for the extra work and doesn't recommend the process unless the soil is deficient and really needs conditioning. The soil in her garden, for example, is in proper condition and is kept that way continually by her mulch. A soil test is a good way of determining whether or not your soil has deficiencies.

Another deficiency that'll do in your plants is a lack of water. As Mrs. Shade learned, the best time to mulch is after a rain. Or, failing that, after the soil has been watered. A mulch is a good moisture conserver, but it can't conserve what isn't there.

By the same token, however, too much water isn't good either. This is why good drainage is important. A too-wet soil is trouble for a garden, and mulching a too-wet garden is just compounding the problem. If you can't solve the problem of an overabundance of water naturally—as Bob Wandzell did by selecting a slope for his garden to promote runoff—a few drainage ditches might help. This is the solution Cynthia Williamson chose.

"Ruth Stout had been talking about mulching humus-rich sandy land," said the Michigan mulcher, "and I was going to mulch humus-poor, heavy soil. Although I realized it would take two or three years for the mulch to condition the earth, I failed to realize that my heavily compacted soil was badly in need of drainage ditches in the lower end.

"Our part of Michigan has had extremely heavy rainfall. After a 4-inch downfall, when the water stood in pools around my transplants of lettuce, tomatoes, peppers and cabbages, it dawned on me I had problems. At the site of an old compost pile, the soil crumbled like moist, light cake; but in the lower end of my 50-by-100-foot garden, the soil was extremely heavy and fell off the spade in tight, wet clods.

"This lower area of the garden had grown tomatoes for two years. The vines had been beautiful and lush with fruit, but frost had hit before a majority could ripen. Previously I had blamed their late maturity on a heavy layer of mulch, but after reading that tomatoes ripen faster on a light, humusy soil I began to wonder. Green peppers had the same trouble. There was plenty of fruit on the vines, but they just didn't grow or ripen rapidly. Perhaps I was too hasty in mulching the entire garden without first enriching the soil's humus content.

"Although tomatoes and peppers had plagued me, other vegetables did well in this area surrounded by mulch. Green peas planted in mid-July stretched up and bore heavily. Late cabbages did well, even though I fed them nothing but a little compost at the start. Now that the area is well-drained, my head lettuce and leaf lettuce grow in abundance, unaffected by the heavy soil, and mulched thickly," she said.

Are there mistakes you can make? Sure there are. But the biggest one you can make is to refuse or to neglect to mulch your garden—or to give up on mulching after one less than abundantly successful try. There's more to mulch than meets the eye. A successful mulch garden may not come overnight. Humus-poor soil won't be rejuvenated in one growing season, so don't expect too much that first year, or the second, for that matter.

Rather, weigh the experiences of others. Test your soil, study its strengths and weaknesses. Consider your climate. Investigate the various mulch material available to you locally in abundance. Then, observing the guidelines and existing conditions, set up a program.

Then get out there and mulch!!!

Appendix I

CALENDAR GUIDE for SEASONAL MULCHING

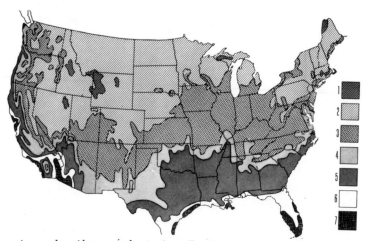

Average date of last expected spring frosts: Zone 1, June; zone 2, May 10-30; zone 3, April 10 to May 10; zone 4, March 20 to April 10; zone 5, February 28 to March 10; zone 6, February 8-28; zone 7, January 30 to February 8.

FEBRUARY: Turn over cover crops and spring weeds and cover the soil with mulch immediately if you are in an arid or drought area. In all other areas the spring crop will grow faster if you leave the soil uncovered for a week or two to warm up before you apply the spring mulch.

After the snow melts in the northern areas, check the mulch in your flower gardens and loosen it where it has become packed down during the winter.

In Zones 2 and 3, start removing the mulch from spring-flowered bulb beds.

In Zone 6, remove mulch from roses, and allow the soil to bake for a couple of weeks before you apply a mulch of new materials. Use the old mulch to enrich the compost pile.

MARCH: In Zone 4 and northward, shred old asparagus plants with either the lawn mower or shredder and return them as a mulch. Mulch half the asparagus bed heavily with a fine material such as cocoa bean shells, well ground corncobs or partly broken down leaf mold. Let the other half of the bed unmulched until shoots begin to break through the mulched half. This extends the asparagus season, because the unmulched part of the bed will begin to bear one to two weeks earlier than the mulched part.

In orchards, pulverized rock fertilizers can be spread below the trees and berry bushes. Work the materials into the top layer of soil before covering it with the summer mulch.

In northern perennial beds, loosen the leaf mulch as soon as the snow has melted, but don't remove this winter mulch too soon. One of its purposes is to keep the ground frozen until it will remain permanently thawed. In Zone 4, work into the soil any manure that remains on the surface around roses, and allow the sun to bake the soil for a couple of weeks before you apply the summer mulch.

APRIL: The winter mulch should be off your planting rows by now, even if you had a dry, snowless winter. Give the spring sun a chance to warm the soil and bring it to life. Later, as the season advances, pull this rather thin mulch back to the row, and add to it as much as you can.

Be shrewd about your mulching. Delay it as long as you safely can in order to warm the soil, without losing too much moisture.

Mulch is more important in the hot Southwest than possibly elsewhere. Residents there should mulch their azaleas and camellias thoroughly with compost or leaf mold, keeping them well watered, especially while they are putting forth new growth after flowering.

In Zone 3, when tomatoes can safely be set out without protection, draw a hay mulch up to the stem of each plant.

In all sections of the country, use the early grass clippings for mulch. These are very rich in nitrogen in this season.

In the orchard spread nitrogen-rich fertilizers around fruit trees and berry bushes if you have not already done so. Cover the fertilizer with a thick mulch of hay, preferably alfalfa.

MAY: Planting will be underway by now and your mulching should be, too. In Zones 4–7, planting must be done immediately for summer crops. When plants are four to five inches high, apply a mulch at least three inches deep. Use old sawdust, hay, leaves, pine needles, or rocks to hold moisture, lessen weed growth and cut down on labor. For these zones, the importance of mulching cannot be overstressed. Continue to gather mulching materials to replenish the ground cover.

In Zones 1 and 2, the winter mulch will have come off a bit later, but the spring soil conditioning program should be nearing completion and some hardier plants should be planted by mid-month. Almost all planting should be done by the beginning of June.

JUNE: Vegetables should be mulched heavily before the dry summer days arrive. You can speed growth for hardier plants by sprinkling cottonseed meal before the new mulch goes on.

JULY: If weeds are starting to push up through your spring mulch, the time has come to spread a few extra bales of hay. The best time to do this is right after a thundershower, when you have fresh moisture to protect. Tiny weeds can be smothered out with hay—no need to pull them first. Draw the mulch up close to the stems of plants like tomatoes, peppers, eggplant and corn. When spreading it next to lettuce, cover the ground first with newspaper and save yourself an extra-difficult washing job later.

AUGUST: Even if you started with newspaper, you may find it pays now to tuck straw and hay around the plants in the row. As for the paths and middles, you can use whatever comes handy to keep the soil from crusting and becoming trodden.

In the vegetable garden, check the mulch in the planting rows and patches to make sure it is not running too thin. Shade the compost pile this month with a thick layer of straw mulch.

Tomatoes may need a fresh layer of mulch at this

time. In the orchard, if a thick mulch has been maintained under the trees all season, it might help the pest situation to rake it away and supply a fresh mulch.

SEPTEMBER: Start now to collect organic materials for winter mulching or for sheet composting. As fast as garden rows are emptied, cover them with layers of materials that will break down during the winter, and that can be turned under in spring. Shredded leaves, fresh manure, hops, apple and castor bean pomace, ground corn cobs, bean and peanut shells are among the materials obtainable in the fall.

OCTOBER: In the North, azaleas and rhododendrons should be mulched with leaves. Central states gardeners should haul back the mulch six to eight inches from the trunks of fruit trees and grapevines.

Mulch Jerusalem artichokes with a thick layer of leaves as soon as soil has a frozen crust. The leaves will prevent hard freezing, and you should be able to push back any snow and to dig tubers at any time during the coming winter. Fall carrot plantings may be treated the same way in all but the very coldest areas.

New strawberry beds can be started at any time from now until midwinter in Zones 5, 6, and 7. Mulch the rows with clean, new straw after planting.

In Zones 1 and 2, mulch peonies with rich manure as soon as the ground freezes. Also cover the rock garden with evergreen boughs as soon as cold weather arrives to stay. This will anchor the snow, so essential to the health of Alpines.

In the orchard, push back mulch six to eight inches from the bases of the fruit trees to discourage rodents that plan to build their winter nests there.

NOVEMBER: Mulch heeled-in fruit trees that have arrived too late from the nursery to be planted. Mulch with straw after the soil is frozen ringing hard, so that the mulch does not harbor field mice.

Clear up all fallen fruit and old leaves, before applying a new fall mulch of leaves. Allow the ground cover to extend beyond the drip-line, but leave a bare area one foot wide around the trunk of each tree to foil the mice. Weigh down the new mulch with large, flat rocks. This procedure is particularly recommended for stone fruits suffering from gummosis.

Otherwise, spread rich manure under the trees and shrubs when they are dormant, covering it immediately with straw, hay or wood-chip mulch. This prevents ammonia from escaping, and will also give winter rains or melting snow a chance to leach it down to the plant roots. Again, leave a one-foot center well open around each tree trunk to prevent damage.

Give the berry bushes a good layer of wood chips, manure, sawdust, or shredded leaves. Blueberries must have an acid mulch—oak leaves are fine—but the others are not so particular.

Compost piles in Zones 4 and 5 can be kept active all winter by mulching them heavily with hay or straw.

For roses whose hardiness may be doubtful, build an overcoat of burlap stretched around 4 posts to surround each bush, and fill the enclosure with a mulch of chopped corn cobs.

Be sure to inspect winter mulches after each heavy windstorm.

MULCHING SOME SPECIFIC PLANTS

Vegetables

ARTICHOKE

Artichokes, Jerusalem or otherwise, thrive under a good light mulch with lots of nitrogen and a moist, well-drained soil. Any nitrogen-rich mulch material will do. Its thickness should be increased as the growing season progresses. The tops can be used as a winter mulch after the vegetables are harvested.

ASPARAGUS

Like most garden plants, asparagus thrives when properly mulched. In the spring you might want to take your nitrogen-rich grass clippings and save them for the asparagus bed. Sometimes it's a good idea to divide your asparagus bed in half. Mulch half the bed heavily with a fine material such as cocoa bean shells, ground corn cobs or partly decomposed leaf mold. Leave the other half unmulched until shoots begin to break through the mulched half. This technique will extend the asparagus season, because the unmulched part of the bed will begin to bear one or two weeks earlier than the mulched part.

At any rate, mulching your asparagus bed will keep it weed free if you use available organic material such as old hay, leaves, straw, salt hay and dried grass clippings—about eight inches for a season. If you want a steady, yearly supply of thick, delicious spears, you repeat that practice every spring.

When you finish your asparagus planting, sometime in late spring or early summer, weed the bed thoroughly, feed it and give it a thick mulch blanket. For the winter, mulch asparagus thickly with fresh manure or compost and allow the top to stand until spring.

One organic gardener, Brownson Malsch of Texas, tried experimenting with cotton-burr mulch on his asparagus beds. It's a material that's handy there and, like most natural materials, it breaks down readily and turns to a mellow compost. The material's obtained directly from the cotton gin, spread several inches deep making for easier maintenance of the planting site. It's rich brown appearance gives an attraction to the planting area while it controls weed growth at the same time.

BEANS

Like most plants in the garden, beans will respond favorably when mulched. Perhaps the most serious cultivating problem in growing beans is the control of weeds. The bean roots are often close to the surface and any deep or extensive cultivation to halt the weeds will result in undesirable root pruning. But a heavy mulch will work for you in keeping down the weeds and give you an added plus in preserving moisture in times of drought. Gardeners have mulched beans successfully with grass clippings and oat straw. The result will be some healthy looking plants and some mighty good eating.

BEETS

Beets are alkaline soil plants, and won't grow in acid soil. It is wise, then, to load your mulch with alkaline materials or use some ground limestone. A light mulch should be applied immediately after planting to conserve moisture and prevent the sun from baking the soil. When sprouts appear, pull the mulch back somewhat. As the growing season progresses, increase the thickness of the mulch and tuck it in close to the maturing plants. Beets thrive in a humus-rich soil, and a continuous mulch will contribute to this condition in your soil.

BROCCOLI

Broccoli should be well-mulched to preserve moisture. Organic gardener Joan Pierson used matted leaves with excellent results. She applied forkfuls of the leaves between the rows of plants, checked a substantial weed and insect problem and produced superb broccoli. Another Joan—Lindeman in this case—uses hay mulch with similar results.

CABBAGE

Spread some mulch on your cabbage bed and watch the cabbage respond. Near the Grand River in Eaton

Rapids, Michigan, Charles Carter grew 18 jumbo heads of cabbage—one of them a real tape measure gem. Carter used rabbit manure as fertilizer and irrigated with river water he brought to his garden with a small electric pump. The mulching was supplied by a nearby sawmill which gave out sawdust just for the asking. When the Carters began harvesting their cabbages, they discovered one head measured 52 inches around and tipped the scale at 35 pounds.

Others have used grass clippings and hay on cabbages with good results.

One of the most surprising mulches that's good for cabbages is aluminum foil. Investigation at Connecticut and other university experimental stations indicated that cabbage mulched with strips of aluminum foil were able to repell disease-carrying aphids and return the increased yields over unprotected plants.

If you live in a warm climate location and one that normally experiences mild winters you might like to plant seeds of cabbages and cover the beds with a coarse mulch during the early winter months like November or early December. Recover the bed with a coarse mulch such as twigs or pine boughs as soon as seedlings appear. In spring when you uncover them, you will have some hardy babies for early transplanting.

CARROTS

When you sow carrots you will probably want to place some mulch over the beds to prevent the soil surface from crusting so that sprouting seeds can't break through. Cover the soil with a little loose hay or other mulch (not so deep as you might normally use it), and water it carefully so that the fine seeds will not wash away. When the slender seedlings come up be certain the mulch doesn't interfere with them.

If you're tired of the pesky brown worm that spoils your carrots you might be able to foil it with a coffee break. Mix your package of carrot seed with one cup of fresh unused coffee grounds. Plant the coffee with your seeds. It percolates enough coffee odor during the growing season to foil the noisiest of carrot flies. And it won't flavor the carrots as sprays and other poisonous substances do. Because coffee grounds are acid, they are good for plants that like that kind of treatment. Often it is best to mix ground limestone with the grounds before using it as a mulch or top-dressing. They seem to have a remarkable effect on stimulating the growth and health of certain plants. Chemical analyses show that the grounds contain small amounts of all sorts of minerals—including trace elements—plus carbohydrates, sugars and even some vitamins, as well as caffeine.

One gardener has found that he likes to leave carrots in the ground during the winter months. By covering them well with a thick mulch he finds that the carrots may be kept that way. At any rate, he prefers it to the frozen or canned carrots that are available in most supermarkets.

CELERY

Ohio gardener Lucille Eisman reports that leaf celery protected with a deep mulch almost covering the plants, will produce crisp, tender hearts until Thanksgiving time or later. Recently she took eight or ten celery plants, complete with roots and a clump of soil and stacked them upright in an unused cold frame. Dried leaves were packed around and between the big plants and gave full protection from the cold.

CORN

When it comes to planting delicious sweet corn, organic gardeners are of one accord—mulching is important. Often it may be best to mulch sparingly—if at all —early, because it's best to let the corn get a good start and allow the soil to warm up. However, if the weather is very dry at planting time you might want to mulch each hill with a handful of old hay or dry grass clippings and remove it as soon as there are signs of germination. Another reason for early mulching could be an abundance of crows in your vicinity. Crows will pull small corn plants nearly as fast as they show above ground. The solution is a thorough mulch that will give the plants a chance to get well started before the crows can spot them. By that time, any plant pulled will yield disappointing results to the average crow, who is after the tender young kernels below the plants.

C. E. Chamberlain of Tacoma, Washington is one of the advocates of mulching growing corn. Chamberlain uses grass clippings that have rotted all winter and mixes them with peat moss and foil. After planting the corn he tops the bed by filling it with a ring of fresh, green grass clippings. He surrounds the plants with 24" circles of inexpensive aluminum grass edging. Edward P. Morris uses a more standard technique of hilling the corn six to eight inches high. Then he uses baled or old spoiled hay which he has shaken out in the area to make a continuous mulch five to six inches deep. He claims it is always wise to work with the wind at your back to keep the dust and seeds away. Sometimes the hay separates quickly and easily into one inch pads or slates which are equal to five or six inches of shaken hay.

CUCUMBERS

Leaves, grass clippings, old hay, leaf mold or other organic mulch all rank high in controlling cucumbers, as does aluminum foil. In fact, mulch could be the way to control the old cucumber nemesis, the cucumber beetle. E. M. Watson of Chardon, Ohio, knows the difference that mulching makes in that regard. "One year I was setting watermelon plants and was driven in by the rain before I could finish," he said. "I had all but one hill mulched with compost. I didn't get back for two days and the unmulched hill was literally destroyed by striped cucumber beetles. The others were not bothered. I had this experience with other things I have mulched; they appeared to be less susceptible to pests."

Down in Houston, Texas, Pat Patterson has found that cucumbers benefit greatly from an organic mulch. When the cucumbers are about three inches in height, Patterson spreads a reservoir of leaves around the tiny plants. Every few days he will add another thin layer of leaves until the mulch is about four inches thick. When an occasional indomitable weed pokes through the mulch, it is easily plucked from the loose soil. If you use lawn clippings as a mulch, let them dry a few days, then apply a four-inch thick layer down the whole row of cucumbers. Actually, any organic mulch will serve as well. It is a good idea to provide mulch wherever cucumber roots might extend, even on the other side of a fence or tree. Look for big improvements in your cucumber patch after you begin to use an organic mulch.

EGGPLANT

Mulches are valuable to the eggplant because it cannot be disturbed if it is to have proper development. Besides smothering the weeds, a good organic mulch will help to conserve a uniform supply of moisture which in turn will enable the roots to feed in the top, moist two inches of soil with which they are surrounded.

GARLIC

Add garlic to the list of plants that get a boost from mulch. Harry Schoth of Corvallis, Oregon grows giant garlic, and he knows the value of using organic material. Schoth welcomes all the grass clippings, weeds and leaves his neighbors care to donate in the fall. Then he maintains two big piles of grass clippings available as mulch during the dry August months. When his garlic is six to eight inches high, Schoth works compost into the soil and mulches with grass clippings between the rows.

KOHLRABI

Moisture is of the greatest importance in feeding kohlrabi for the best growth. A thick mulch should be drawn up to the seedlings as soon as they are tall enough, and the soil beneath the mulch should be kept moist. One experienced kohlrabi grower, Dexter Raymond, uses hay, grass clippings and pulled weeds to mulch his plants. Ruth Stout uses hay rather success-fully.

LEEKS

Leeks profit from mulches of all sorts, including peat, straw, compost, wood shavings and autumn leaves. Be certain that when mulching young seedlings the mulch doesn't interfere with them as they sometimes come up rather thick in the seed bed.

LETTUCE

Lettuce is a plant which needs a coarse mulch material such as twigs or pine burrows in the seedling bed. If you already have a planting area that has seen the mulch break down a bit in early summer, scatter some lettuce seed there. The lettuce appreciates the semi-shade as well as the rich, rotting mulch.

If you have to plant your lettuce after the chill of early spring, apply a thin straw mulch around and right up underneath the lettuce leaves. This does three things: holds soil moisture; keeps the large leaves off damp soil to prevent rot; maintains the cool root run that many plants (especially cool season vegetables) require for best production. Aluminum foil also has been used suc-cessfully as a lettuce mulch.

OKRA

In growing okra, a good mulch is important if your soil is heavy and rain abundant. Before the plants bloom, work the aisles. Hill the growing plants and mulch between the rows heavily with straw, old hay or well-rotted cow manure. Mulch the rows themselves lightly—just enough to discourage weeds but not the okra—since this plant needs plenty of warmth. Grass clippings are ideal for this light mulch. Other gardeners have found that leaves—even oak leaves—are good for mulching okra.

ONIONS

Mulch will aid the first stages of onion growth and maintain the plants during cold weather. Don't put much stock in the rumors that onions don't appreciate mulching. Mrs. Paul Gillette of Shelton, Washington reports that she put several inches of fresh fir sawdust on her onions and had the biggest and best she ever saw. Gordon Snyder of Glidden, Wisconsin plants his onions in spring—plowed ground under a two-inch mulch of kiln-dried hardwood shavings. That's all the work he does and he has been taking first prize for onions at the local country fair for several years. Ruth Stout has always claimed that her hay mulched onions are extremely mild and good eating. Walter Starns of Bethel, New York, echoes Mr. Snyder's statement on kiln-dried sawdust and shavings with Spanish onions. "It will", he says, "definitely produce larger winter onions."

PARSNIPS

To prolong the use of fresh garden parsnips, heap leaves high over the rows as cold weather moves in. These leaves will prevent the soil from freezing, and enable you to pull fresh vegetables from the ground long after the rest of the garden freezes solid.

PEAS

Trying to grow peas all summer is a rather hopeless gamble unless the most important growing principle is observed—mulch early and mulch deeply. Use straw or any material that's handy but be sure it is put on as soon as the seeds are sown—rather thin at first, then more heavily as the plants get started. Provide a deep buffer of mulch between the heat of the atmosphere and the soil. The cool, moist root run is the important difference between success or failure of summer-long peas.

Ruth Tirrell knows that peas must go in early, and the soil has to be ready to receive them. That's why an early mulching program includes plenty of organic material that gets incorporated into the soil usually the autumn before. Leaves or other clean debris are dug in and a mulch of similar material is put down for the winter. The result is enriched, productive soil that yields high quality vegetables. After the peas are planted she draws back the winter mulch to the furrow. It could cover the latter loosely. Because peas are a coarse plant they will come up through it. By the time the peas are pulled up the winter mulch will have just about disappeared. If you can, renew the mulch. Use grass clippings, hay, straw, weeds or the nitrogen-rich pea vines themselves. The mulch of organic material will prevent root rot, a disease to which peas on poorly drained land are susceptible.

PEPPERS

Peppers respond well to mulching. Most any good organic material, such as hay or grass clippings will do. But if you want early-ripening peppers, use a tar-paper mulch in conjunction with glass cloches to permit planting the peppers two to three weeks earlier than you normally would. Use a good-quality tar paper since this will be a mulch to use and reuse for years. Cut 18-inch squares of the tar paper and put a five inch hole in the center of each. Place the tar paper over the ground with the plant growing through the hole. Cover the plant with the cloche, which can be made by cutting the bottoms of one-gallon clear glass jugs.

The tar paper mulch will collect the heat of the day and help maintain it through the night. It will keep the ground moist, although it won't contribute anything nutritional to the soil. The individual greenhouses will allow the peppers to get the sunlight and still be protected from late spring frosts.

When the pepper plant fills the cloche, remove it and the tar paper and put down an organic mulch.

POTATOES

Probably no other garden plant is more synonymous with mulching than potatoes. You can grow potatoes under mulch, in mulch, on top of mulch—almost any way in fact—and get satisfactory results.

Generally, planting potatoes on top of any mulch remaining from last season is effective. After they are set in rows, cover the eyed pieces with at least 6 to 8 inches of hay, straw or other loose material. If soil stays cold in your area during early spring, try a delayed mulch. To harvest early potatoes, remove hay or straw carefully when blossoms start falling, separate small potatoes from stems, and generally replace mulch. One organic gardener planted potatoes on top of the ground in a cover of leaves. The leaves are piled over the potato patch the previous fall to a depth of three feet and left there for the winter. By spring they are packed down and earthworms are working through them. Potatoes are planted by laying the pieces directly on the leaves in rows where they are to grow. The seed is then covered with 12 to 14 inches of hay or straw. More mulch is added later, if tubers appear through the first. When harvest time comes, the mulch is pulled back and

Early potatoes are harvested from their thick bed of mulch, then covering is replaced.

potatoes are picked and put into their sacks with no digging necessary.

Don Tillung of Deerfield, Wisconsin, uses a method of raising potatoes on top of the ground which eliminates a lot of labor. His mulch cover is eight inches of marsh hay—usually the cheapest type. If the soil is high in nitrogen content, the hay on the bottom of the mulch will tend to decay rapidly which may require more to maintain a minimum of eight inches. Advantages are that you don't have to cultivate and you don't have bothersome potato bugs.

Edith Sarwell of Lake Forest, Illinois uses a straw mulch to plant her potatoes. The mulch keeps the soil cold and could cause a late maturity—if that's what you are after. Or, why not try two plantings—a very early one for a good head start and another in July for winter and spring harvesting. If hay or leaves are not available in your locality, try to cover each potato row with an eight-inch layer of pine needles. It makes a light, airy mulch and keeps moisture down under the needles. That will make the earthworms mighty happy and the potatoes mighty good eating.

There's one sure mulching method that controls the potato bug. It was conceived and tested at the Organic Gardening Experimental Farm. The potato seeds must be planted and the soil covered with a one-foot layer of hay or straw mulch. Through experiments it was determined that the hay is the better of the two. The plants, of course, will grow through this mulch, but the potato bug, whose egg winters in the soil, cannot climb up on the potato stem through the heavy mulch. This method of heavy mulching proved so effective that not a single potato bug could be found on the potato plant. At the end of the season the mulch is plowed under, thus enriching the soil with valuable organic matter and giving it a better structure. The plants also benefit from this highly successful method, for they obtain a greater health and resistance to insects and disease.

Kenneth Polscer discovered that potatoes planted in soil and mulched with hay give better results than potatoes mulched with plastic. The hay keeps down the weeds, and can be turned under to decompose in the soil and provide added nutrients, something plastic can never do.

PUMPKINS

Pumpkins will profit from hay from a newly-mowed field. Mulch around each hill. Before laying down the mulch, work in a feeding of cow manure.

In Troy, New York a group of youngsters discovered that composted leaves, old hay, straw, cow manure and bone meal gave forth insect-free pumpkins that had no trouble from dryness. "From now on," says Joe Miller, "we're growing everything in the garden in organic compost."

RADISHES

Donald Shaw of Colona, Illinois planted white winter radishes on the Fourth of July, and mulched them with chopped, partly-decayed clover hay as soon as they were high enough. The results more than pleased Shaw, as one of the radishes scaled 6 pounds and measured 28 inches long.

"We ate the smaller ones—those that weighed only a pound or two each!" Shaw said.

RHUBARB

Thick stalks of rhubarb result from continuous heavy feeding. To keep the soil up to the standard necessary, spread a thick mulch of strawy manure over the bed after the ground freezes in winter. Nutrients will be leached into the soil during the winter. In spring, rake the residue aside to allow the ground to warm and the plants to sprout. Then draw the residue together with a thick new blanket of straw mulch up around the plants. Hay, leaves or sawdust also make excellent mulches for rhubarb. A side benefit of the sawdust and leaves is that they contribute to the acidity of the soil, and rhubarb thrives in an acid soil.

SPINACH

Spinach can be mulched with grass clippings, hay or ground corncobs and it will be the better for it. Inez Grant of Columbia, Maine has used hay successfully. Since spinach doesn't grow well in acid soil, acidic mulches such as sawdust or leaves shouldn't be used. Summer mulches shouldn't be applied until the leaves have made a good growth.

SQUASH

Squash needs an extra special dose of mulch, particularly during hot, dry summers. Try a heavy dousing of compost and rotted sawdust. Make your mulch as much as four inches deep. Aluminum foil mulch has been found to repel aphids from squash plants.

SWEET POTATOES

Sweet potatoes are heavy feeders, and they grow well when they have sufficient moisture. A good mulch cover with compost will fill both of those requirements. Old leaves and grass clippings on the sides of the rows make an adequate mulch, as do the old standbys—hay and straw. If you make a hill for your sweet potatoes, be sure you mulch them well, allowing plenty of room for them to develop. At season's end, work the mulch deeply into the soil to build up humus content.

TOMATOES

Deep mulching and delicious tomatoes go hand in hand. Organic gardeners have been experiencing great results for years with mulching. Take the case of Robert E. English of Baltimore, Maryland. He mulches his plants when they reach sufficient size. If leaves are handy, they are used to a height of four inches or more, but with grass clippings or sawdust the plants may be somewhat smaller. Much of his mulching is done following a storm, using leaves, since they are not shredded. Either grass, sawdust or old rugs are used to hold the leaves in place. With every passing year English has found his soil easier to spade and the number of earthworms on the increase. He believes his use of mulch has contributed greatly to the soil fertility. Frank and Cecile Fiederlein of Cape Cod have found success in mulching their tomato plants with leaves and pine needles. "The tomatoes were the envy of the neighborhood. Besides having enough for our family and friends, my wife put up fifty-five quarts for the winter," Fiederlein said.

Fruits

BANANAS

Oliver R. Franklin of Fort Myer, Florida, showed his neighbors that organic mulch methods could revive banana growing. "They told me that bananas did poorly here," he said, "and from the looks of those growing in nearby yards, it appears believable. However, I planted mine in the same kind of soil, but shocked the neighbors by capturing islands of water hyacinths floating by in the river, and pitching them ashore with a hay fork and mulching the bananas a foot deep with them. I figured that the rains had washed a lot of soluble minerals and trace elements into the river to be captured by the weeds, and I wanted some of it back.

"When the hyacinths decayed around the bananas, I mulched them deeply with the most aged shavings and sawdust I could find. The plants responded by growing twice as tall as their parent stock, with none of the usual root rot and no insect pests."

BLUEBERRIES

Although blueberry plants, like most other harborages of the garden, profit from mulch, it's best to be a bit wary about how much and what you use. When setting out blueberries, the soil pH should be between 4.5 and 5.0. By applying organic mulches—never any lime—you'll be able to keep it that way. Peat moss, hard wood, leaves, pine needles, and similar materials decompose into an acid compost-mulch. Also good is sphagnum moss or shredded oak leaves. If the pH is unusually low, the mulch may be composed of shredded corn cob. Use saw dust as a mulch only if it has been composted with manure for at least a year.

Don't go hog wild mulching blueberries. When plants are first set out, a three to four inch mulch around the plant or about one inch over the whole plot is adequate. Increase the depth as the plants grow to a maximum of six to eight inches. Although mulching may prevent many bacterial and fungus diseases, over-mulching could open a Pandora's box of problems, particularly if the soil is poorly drained, making blueberries more susceptible to disease.

Frank Fiederlein of Cape Cod is a blueberry mulcher who has had success using pine needles, sawdust, some decayed leaves and sand. Around the roots he uses a mixture of sand, loam and peat moss. Each year he adds a two inch layer of pine needles. He reports that his yields are getting bigger all the time.

BOYSENBERRIES

Ethel M. Stephens of California has found that boysenberries profit from organic mulch. Because boysenberries are terrific feeders, a mulch of well rotted compost or leaves does a good job. Ethel has found that after many years of that treatment, her soil has become a deep, soft mass of organic material that holds moisture like a sponge. In hot, dry weather she mulches partially rotted sawdust to further conserve moisture and humus surrounding the roots.

CANTALOUPES

Cantaloupes and other melons need lots of moisture from the time they come up until they are nearly full-grown. For this reason, they'll do better under a thick mulch. The best materials to use include hay, grass clippings, shells and hulls and newspapers. Stay away from sawdust and leaves, since these materials may add too much acid to the soil for the alkaline-loving melons.

The mulch should be put down before the fruit develop, since handling may damage the tender melons. Once the melons do develop, they'll be resting on a clean carpet of mulch and won't be prone to rot.

CITRUS TREES

Mulch under a citrus tree should be kept at least eight inches from the base of the tree so it doesn't foster root rot. Keep the mulch pulled well back and don't allow any irrigation water to stand at the foot of the tree.

Bearing this caution in mind, there are few things more beneficial for a citrus tree than a good mulch. One California orchardist allows the trees to mulch themselves. He just never rakes up the leaves that fall from the trees. Other orchardists grow the mulch material within the orchard itself. Summer cover crops that may be planted in the orchard and cut for mulching material include soybeans, cowpeas, millet, sudan grass and buckwheat. Winter cover crops that can be cut for mulching include rye, wheat, vetch, clover, alfalfa and kudzu beans.

Growing the mulching material in the orchard is a practice which stemmed from the large amount of material needed to properly mulch such an area. An orchardist thus doesn't have to reserve areas free of trees for cultivating mulching materials, nor does he have to purchase materials. Both of these practices continue, however. Besides the various grasses that may be used for mulching materials, you can use sawdust, weeds, peat, corncobs, brewery and canning wastes, rotten wood and leaves and, of course, stones.

Tests in New Zealand have indicated that citrus trees under mulch are healthier and produce better fruit than those not mulched. In addition, the mulched trees need only half as much fertilizer as unmulched ones. Similar tests in the United States have demonstrated that mulched trees come into bearing sooner than trees under clean cultivation. Mulches are particularly beneficial for trees between one and four years old, since these trees are most sensitive to competition from other vegetation.

FIGS

Like all fast-growing tropical plants, the fig responds quickly to a good mulch. A heavy mulch in summer to retain moisture, and in the winter to protect against the weather, plus a spring application of good compost, will usually guarantee even growth. A tree so treated needs no cultivation.

FRUIT TREES

Organic mulches are highly recommended in starting and growing fruit trees, particularly the dwarf variety. After the trees begin to grow, add a shovelful of well-rotted manure around each tree. Then mulch thoroughly. Apply the mulch to conserve moisture and aid new root growth. If you use straw, apply one half to one bale per tree. Other materials that can be used include compost and leaf mold or hay. Keep all mulches

Flat stones should be used to anchor mulch around young fruit trees.

away from the base of the trunk to discourage rodents which can damage trees severely. Stone or stone chips might make an effective mulch, keep weeds down and deter animal pests. If your fruit trees are growing in a bare, recently pulled orchard, spread a mulch over the root area in late fall before temperatures tumble. You may not be able to regulate the winter blasts that sweep the branches and kill the bugs, but you can preserve your orchard for another year.

Keep in mind that your soil needs to be kept moist (not wet). A soil kept wet invites stagnation which leads to root rot. Water once, then get down to the business of mulching. The mulch is especially important during the first growing season, whether transplanting is done in autumn or spring. The mulch conserves soil moisture, but it also keeps the soil cool under the hot summer sun. Moisture and coolness are equally important in promoting vigorous root growth. Whenever rainfall is scant (naturally or unusually) a thorough soaking of the soil every two or three weeks will keep the trees growing as if there were no drought.

And if you have summer showers, you can make better use of them by mulching. This prevents thorough drying for a time. If you have scattered large rocks on top of the soil under the mulch, they act as condensers to return rising moisture to the depths. But the greatest soil moisture loss is through transpiration of the leaves, and this is one thing that you do not want to prevent, because it is necessary for their growth.

Mrs. C. F. Brock of Jay, Oklahoma has found that mulching her peach trees with maple leaves was just what they needed. "In the fall two years ago, I carried six sacks of maple leaves and dumped them into the place I had spaded out along the peach trees, (mixing several spades-full of rotted manure in the soil), and since I did not have rocks to cover the leaves, I used old brick on top and around the edges.

"My husband laughed at me—but when the peaches were ripe, he didn't laugh any more. He never saw such large well formed peaches and the nice part about it was there were no webs. Those mouth-watering luscious peaches made a believer out of him. He mulched all his fruit trees this fall."

GRAPES

Grapes deserve mulching, even the first year. Alfalfa hay and sand-straw-steer manure mixture rank high on the list of mulch-fertilizer combinations. Before the rainy season is the best time for the overall spread of mulches and various manures. If you choose hay or shredded leaves, work additional nutriment into the soil. It might be best to use compost, wood ashes or granite dust as fertilizer.

LOGANBERRIES

Sawdust mulching greatly increases cane growth and yields as compared to clean cultivation.

MOCK ORANGE

During the hot days of summer, it is well to use a mulch three to four inches thick for the mock orange tree. Put it on after a thorough watering and use different materials. Whether it be composed of vegetable matter from a compost pile, manure or leaf mold, all would

167

be suitable. Although some mulches are at the same time top dressings, they also prevent over-rapid evaporation, and enrich the soil by furnishing new food to the shrub.

PAPAYA

Edwin H. Avrims saved an untreated papaya tree by using a large quantity of mulch. The tree had been uprooted by a heavy wind and it was decided to destroy the tree as its roots were largely out of the ground. But instead, the tree was propped up at an angle of some 30 or 40 degrees and loads of compost and garden soil placed over the roots until it was well covered. When it was found that the tree was still alive and even putting out new branches while burring heavily, more and more mulch was added from time to time, and it made a surprising comeback. It not only matured a large crop of food that it carried when overthrown, but actually put out several tree limbs and grew a large crop of good-sized fruit on these in addition.

RASPBERRIES

Sawdust and wood chips make an excellent mulch for raspberries and have increased production in Canadian tests as much as 50 per cent. Apply a sawdust or chip mulch about three or four inches thick to the base of the plants. The mulch will save moisture, cut down weeds and raise yields. Browned corn stalks and poultry litter also make a good raspberry mulch as do decomposed leaves when used as deep as five inches.

Jean Bowman of Pennsylvania says that she hasn't needed direct fertilizer applications in many years.

"But," she writes, "we have mulched at one time or another with pine needles, sawdust, grass clippings, oak leaves and wood chips. These have decomposed and have enriched the soil, conserved moisture, shaded the ground and smothered most of the weeds. Beth Criteser of Roseburg, Oregon uses grass clippings and leaves as a mulch and fertilizes all of her garden that way. She had berries more than nine feet up the vine and managed to pick enough for dessert on Thanksgiving Day.

STRAWBERRIES

The very nature of a strawberry makes it both responsive to organic methods and most sadly vulnerable to poisonous sprays. The root system fans out below the crown in a perpendicular pattern rather than a horizontal as so many other plants do. Tiny hair roots scatter in all directions from the main roots in search of nutrition and moisture. Mulch should be well dug in to keep the bottom leaves clear so air can circulate around the plants, otherwise berries will mold on the stem.

If the mulch is allowed to remain fairly late in the spring, the plants will be protected from starting into growth so soon that their blossoms may be frosted. When the weather starts to warm up, watch the plants under the mulch. They will show definite signs of wanting to grow, and the leaves will begin to yellow when they need the sun. This is the time when the mulch should be pulled back, leaving enough straw around the plants to cover the bare soil. Leaves will grow up through this light mulch, which will help to smother the weeds and to keep the berries clean. If a late frost threatens after blossoms have begun to develop, draw the winter mulch back over the plants for the night and remove it in the morning.

The best materials for mulching strawberries are wheat straw, cotton hulls, crushed corncobs, peat moss, wood shavings, pine needles or spoiled hay. Leaves make a good mulching material, particularly if corn stalks or tomato vines are applied first to prevent matting.

Although a good thick mulch will prolong the growing season, all good things have to end sometime. When the pickings dwindle down, spread an inch of young, rich compost around the remaining plants and mulch the beds heavily with clean straw. Draw the mulch up to the plants and, as new runners develop, tuck the most promising under the mulch. When the ground is frozen in fall, recheck your mulch and be sure it is thick enough. If you are using straw or hay, a depth of six inches is not too much, particularly in north central states.

WATERMELON

Watermelon vines may be mulched to keep down the weeds and retain the large amounts of moisture needed by the maturing plants. The mulch shouldn't be applied before the soil has warmed, however. Hoeing will keep the weeds down until the soil is warmed sufficiently to permit mulching. Using straw, hay or chopped leaves, spread a six-inch mulch over the entire watermelon patch, drawing the covering up to the bases of the vines. This should be done before the fruit is formed, since it is tender and easily damaged. The best time to apply the mulch is when the soil is thoroughly dampened. As the watermelons develop, they'll be kept dirt-free by the mulch and won't be prone to rot on the vines.

Ornamentals

ARBORVITAE

As every arborvitae lover knows, winter injury can be a real nemesis. It causes a browning of the previous season's growth in late winter or early spring due to drying winds or hot sun. Trees in exposed locations are more severely affected. This discoloration is due to evaporation of moisture from the leaves or needles faster than the roots can pick up water and it is very apt to occur on newly transplanted trees. A thorough mulching of some heavy material like straw or hay will maintain moisture in the ground and help prevent this disease.

AZALEAS

The importance of mulching azaleas cannot be over-emphasized. The roots are extremely shallow—most of them lie within three or four inches of the surface—and they must be kept moist at all times. Thus a mulch of at least four inches is necessary.

Pine needles, oak leaves and sawdust from oak, cypress or hemlock make excellent mulches. A mixture of materials is preferable since the mulch in decaying continually adds food to the soil. Many growers find that a combination of pine needles and oak leaves is especially good. The needles keep the leaves from blowing and are high in acidity but slow in decaying. The oak leaves decay more rapidly and, while lower in acidity, are higher in food value. Seaweed added to the mulch from time to time adds trace minerals. Manure is not recommended for azaleas because of its alkaline reaction.

Some gardeners have found they're able to bring their azaleas through the winter with much less loss by applying winter mulch early in the fall. One gardener uses four inches of bark dust or sawdust and tills it under every spring. By adding mulch before freezing, he has found most of his plants come up from the roots even if peripheral ones are killed.

Victor A. Carley of Berryville, Arkansas, uses mold or shredded leaves—mostly oak—to revitalize his otherwise hard to handle azaleas and wild orchards. The finely shredded leaves keep the soil conditioned if they are packed around the roots. Robert Couldwig reports that azaleas can be transplanted after being mulched like that, "and you would hardly know they had been moved." The leaves are neat, have no weed seeds, and hold moisture like a sponge, keeping the growth zone cooler in hot weather.

Mulching can be a plus if you are stricken by azalea petal blight, a disease that produces small pale spots on the inner surfaces of the petals of the colored flowers and brown spots on the white flowers. The spots rapidly enlarge until the whole flower collapses. A good preventative technique is covering the azalea beds with several inches of mulching material. That helps keep the arresting structures free of the spores. Avoid overhead watering while the plants are in flower and rely upon the deep mulching instead.

BEGONIAS

Buckwheat hulls are an especially good mulch for tuberous begonias when these moisture-lovers are put into the open ground rather than pots. Tuberous begonias are tender, naturally cool-weather plants, and are heavy feeders. The soil should be cool and moist to make nutrition constantly available, but the soil should not be soggy, which may cause rotting of the tubers. Buckwheat hulls improve the appearance of the begonia bed, and prevent the blossoms from becoming mud-splattered.

BOXWOOD

Boxwood profits from mulching particularly in the fall. Like most evergreens, boxwoods prefer a straw, leaf mold or rotted manure mulch. Such mulches prevent wide fluctuation in soil temperature and help the soil hold moisture. The mulch can be left on all winter, and then worked into the soil in the spring. A newly-planted bush should be mulched to the same depth that prevailed in the nursery or woods.

CHRYSANTHEMUMS

If your winters are not too severe and your mums are hearty, you may want to mulch heavily with straw or hay and leave them out over the winter. The object of this protection is prevention of soil heaving and the resulting root damage. If you leave your mums outdoors over winter, do not confine them to pots, but allow them to bloom naturally in October and November.

173

DAHLIAS

Dahlias will profit from a mulch of dried grass clippings or old hay about six inches deep. Buds form quickly after mulch is applied, so keep that in mind for planting your garden color.

DAISIES

Some nurserymen claim you can carry daisies through the coldest winter if you mulch them with eight inches of straw after the ground freezes. It might be a good technique particularly for gardeners up north who have a tendency to lose these vibrant flowers.

DELPHINIUMS

Delphiniums need a thick mulch of straw and clipped grass to keep the roots cool through the hot summer and to conserve moisture. You might also like to apply a generous amount of wood ashes, particularly if slugs or snails seem overly fond of your new delphinium shoots.

DOGWOODS

Dogwoods profit from a pine straw of leaf mulch three or four inches thick. Avoid making a mound of mulch or soil around the plant, which will shed water away from it, as dogwoods can often use a good drink during dry summer months.

EVERGREENS

Small evergreens, like any other planting, benefit from regular watering, frequent cultivation, or most important, a mulch to help control weeds. You probably will find a heavy mulch between the trees of either compost or rotted manure to be effective. Even as seedlings, evergreens are tough, but the first winter it might be a good idea to tuck a deep layer of straw around each tree. If the straw is sufficiently moist in the fall, they should come through the first winter in fine shape. One organic gardener has found that a heavy mulch of equal parts of leaf mold and cow manure does a good job of preventing deep freezing and also supplies adequate and continuous water. Normally, a heavy leaf mulch, preferably oak leaves which last longer and contribute more to an acid condition, will give your evergreen trees the shot in the arm they need.

FERN

A woodsy location, with shade, moisture, and an organic soil high in leaf mold is perfect for the majority of the ferns. Oak leaves and compost are good substitutes for the leaf mold. Peat moss is also an excellent choice because it contributes to the neatness of the beds and ferns just love its acidity.

FLOWERS

Flowers make up a big category, but generally you may use a mulch to alter the soil texture to suit specific plants. Bulbs like Alpines which require a gritty soil may be accommodated by spreading a fine rock chip mulch over the soil surface. Damp meadow conditions may be simulated by laying perforated water pipes below the surface of the soil. A chopped leaf compost mixed with plenty of rotted manure or cottonseed meal

175

has approximately the texture and nutrients of rich wood soil. If acid spring water is available on the site, a planting of sphagnum moss in it will bring a fine bed for picture plants or bogged orchids. During the June growing months you want to be certain that all your flowers are under mulch. Ground corn cobs are fine for roses, while coffee grounds mixed with about an inch of sawdust make a handsome flower bed mulch. The coarser screenings from the compost heap can also be spread evenly around the flowers.

Texas gardeners have found that cotton burr mulching makes the difference between success and failure. Of course, in that region the material is plentiful as well as effective and it produces humus on the spot. Spread the dried burrs several inches deep around the base of the plants. Cotton burr mulch is light in weight and sufficiently porous so that it will not smother. When spread on flowering plants, the rich brown composted burrs give a neat, attractive appearance to the beds, and control weed growth at the same time.

Most annuals like a late fall planting, even though they are particularly hardy. After the first thaw in your area has penetrated the ground about an inch or so, try a mulch three to six inches thick depending on the severity of your winters. It's probably best to make it a light mulch, such as compost, straw, manure, pine needles, fresh or partly decayed leaves, peat moss or salt hay.

In early spring give consideration to mulching your perennials. If there is plenty of spring rainfall in your area, rake back the mulch to allow the furrow to warm up. But if you are in an area of skimpy rainfall, leave the mulch in place and content yourself with later warming. Before it gets too hot be sure to mulch your perennials with compost and rock fertilizers. To keep the weeds out you might use peat moss—a material which contributes to flower bed neatness as well as making the soil on the acid side.

GLADIOLUS

Do you want to experiment with materials to mulch gladiolus? Florence M. Chase has found that hay is the most satisfactory mulch material since it does not mat and allows the spikes to push through easily, eliminating their chance of being deformed. Normally she mulches to a depth of about five inches, and has had excellent results with discouraging thrip infestation. Cornell University experimenters at Farmingdale, New York have discovered that aluminum foil protects gladiolus from attack by aphids. The researchers have found it highly effective in combating the cucumber mosaic virus, a disease carried from plant to plant by aphids which cause "color break" in flowers and streaking of leaves.

HEATHS

Heaths demand an acid material mulch and will thrive in it. That means you probably should choose an oak leaf mold, sawdust or pine needle mulch and apply it during the early growing season.

HOLLY

Because hollies love water and moisture, be certain to apply a yearly surface mulch of well rotted oak leaf compost or wood leaf mold. Hollies also benefit from a tobacco stem mulch placed over the root area underneath the entire branch spread of the tree. The tobacco stems are rich in nutrients and perhaps detrimental to insects. When fed with a mulch of tobacco stems, hollies respond with darker green leaves and more berries.

In New Jersey, Earl Dilatush reports that oak leaf mulches are essential in growing the bright red-berried holiday greenery. He reports many cases where a heavy mulch of oak leaves has revived and restored failing holly trees.

HYDRANGEA

Pearl Wright has found that plenty of mulch— enough to protect the entire root system of a hydrangea —will get even the most pampered house pet safely through the rigors of a Mid-Illinois winter. She first mulched her hydrangea heavily with straw, working it well along the stem and adding a heavy layer of cow manure. Figuring the manure would act "just as it does in a hot bed", she then covered the whole thing with sacks. When her straw-mulched plant survived, she added potato, apple, pear and banana peelings—in fact, all the kitchen left-overs including meat and egg scraps. It was no wonder that hordes of earthworms could be seen in her hydrangea beds digging around the plant and aerating the soil. If you want to grow good hydrangeas, especially in an area where the temperatures drop to twenty below and stay there, put enough mulch around your plant so that you protect the entire root system. The results of Pearl Wright's growings can't be topped—one fabulous shrub bore 240 blossoms at once.

IRIS

Iris mulch should be applied to the base of the plant where it can control weeds growing in the flower beds. Use any organic matter on hand—sometimes strawberry plants from the old bed or just dry grass clippings. Ruth Stout disproved the old theory that bearded iris can't be mulched. She mulched her iris with loose hay and had profuse blooms as beautiful as any around. If the sun's rays can get through a layer of loose hay to make potatoes green, she concluded, it can obviously penetrate the same mulch on a bed of iris and give the rhizomes the needed treatment. It may be best not to use anything heavy—such as peat moss—she admits, but loose hay is a natural.

LAWNS

There seems to be little doubt that grass seed newly sown will benefit from a cover of mulch. Often straw or old hay maintains enough moisture to allow the seed to germinate. The covering shouldn't be so thick as to prevent the grass from sprouting through as seedlings. Even a light covering of green grass clippings will help grass seed germinate.

The mulching status of already established lawns becomes more controversial, however, because a lawn can mulch itself as it is mowed and there is a great temptation to allow the grass clippings to deteriorate and turn into humus. The theory is that letting the grass clippings remain uncollected will provide for a more fertile soil and a more luxuriant bed of sod. Some gardeners argue, however, that the practice of not collect-

179

ing grass clippings produces a sick thatch that inhibits grass growth and development.

Actually, both schools of thought bear the seeds of truth. If you do the same thing with your grass clippings all the time, you're wrong. Occasionally allow your grass clippings to go back into the soil for added enrichment. But never allow them to accumulate so thickly as to form the underlying thatch.

LILACS

When spring rolls around, spread a six-inch layer of well rotted compost around the lilac bush and out far enough to take in most of the branch spread. Dig that in well, being careful not to injure the root, and cover with a mulch of hay or leaves with ashes, or pine needles if the soil is not acid enough. The lilacs, like most shrubs, grow best in slightly acid soil. If it is too acid, an application of agricultural lime is recommended. In the late fall work that mulch into the soil and remulch with leaves or grass clippings for the winter. That will prevent heaving of roots when the ground freezes and thaws.

LILIES

Lily bulbs must be kept well drained, and yet remain cool and moist. That condition demands a good mulch. Manure may be used over the top of the soil, if it is sufficiently decayed. A deep mulch of leaf mold over the lily bed will be appreciated during the hot weather, although the lilies may be planted among low growing annuals or bushes that will keep the soil shaded. After the first frost, cut your lily plants back to the ground and cover with a light mulch of sawdust to protect new bulbs that are growing on the stem. Later, when the ground is frozen hard, cover with a very thick mulch of hay to pull them through the winter.

PANSY

Pansies want a cool, moist soil and a rich mulch, for they are gluttons. Use manure, compost, woods soil, leaf mold, or sawdust and shavings mixed with sheep or poultry manure. The mulch feeds them richly—they are surface feeders—and keeps the roots cool in summer and warm in winter.

PEONIES

Peonies can profit from a mulch of seaweed if it is available. If not, you might want to use a pine-bark mulch which will leave a nice, red-brown appearance. The pine bark will provide added nutrients to the soil and if you add pigeon manure over the winter you should have all the ingredients necessary for productive peonies.

POINSETTIAS

If you're transferring poinsettias out of doors, be sure you mulch them heavily. Be sure to keep them well mulched with lawn clippings or other good organic mulching material.

ORIENTAL POPPIES

Oriental poppies must be mulched in the fall. However, remove that mulch in the spring and stake them. By removing the mulch in springtime, you allow the soil to warm up and the poppies to provide rich early blooms that will dot your spring garden.

RHODODENDRONS

Leaves and sawdust make excellent mulches for the rhododendron bed, chiefly because these plants need an acidic soil. These plants are subject to chlororis, which stems from too basic a soil condition. The leaves will turn yellow or brown. An acidic mulch is an excellent preventative for this condition, or a good cure, should it occur.

It's usually best to add a winter mulch to rhododendrons before the temperature drops too far. By adding the mulch before freezing, you will help your plants to come up from the roots in spring. Rhododendron roots are fairly delicate and sensitive to soil heaving in winter. Add about four inches of sawdust or leaves in the fall and turn them under in spring.

ROSES

How important is mulch for roses? Frankly, it probably is rather foolhardy to attempt to grow roses without mulching. Horticulturist H. P. Rosen of Wright University in Arkansas says, "One cannot overemphasize the importance of a thick mulch, applied anew each spring as a sanitary measure. Such a mulch acts as an insulating layer that prevents soil-born infectious material from reaching new growth. Perhaps the best mulch is a thick layer of rotted cow manure."

Most roses will probably do twice as well with a mulch as without it, and often with roses a mulch may mean the difference between life and death.

Think about your mulching campaign early in the spring. Perhaps you will want to remove some of the old mulch that has been left to lie from last season. If you buried the top of the roses for winter protection under the mulch, resurrect them gradually. Then tear off the

Mulch can often mean the difference between life or death for roses, here being covered with a blanket of sugar cane.

183

old mulch entirely and work the tired old straw, leaves or whatever you used after it is half decayed into new compost heaps along with the winter's kitchen wastes and some fresh manure. Or if your rose soil is workable, turn the old mulch under right there. It will break down quickly, worked over by all the awakening and newly hatched soil animals, insects and bacteria. Earthworms begin to stir, slugs and snails chew up and break down any coarse mulch, and the spring cleaning of the rose bed is under way. When everything is operating efficiently, blanket the roses with a layer of fresh mulch, and the life of the soil continues to percolate under its brand new cover. Grass clippings from the earliest spring mowings will provide a nitrogen-rich cover. Freshly ground corncobs are fine for roses, while coffee grounds, mixed with about an inch of sawdust, make a handsome flower bed mulch. Shredded pine bark or cocoa bean hull, applied to approximately a two-inch level after spring pruning and seeding have produced excellent results. Even newspaper or sawdust on the rose beds has given excellent results.

Leaves are an excellent mulch for the rose beds, as they prevent alternate thawing and freezing that can destroy delicate root systems. But be careful they do not mat over the crowns, or crown rot will result. When leaves are used, the plants should be four or more inches in height; when using grass clippings or sawdust, the plants can be somewhat smaller. It's a good idea to mulch following a storm, using leaves, unless they are shredded. Use either grass, sawdust, or even old rugs to hold the leaves in place. Where sawdust is placed directly on the soil, pigeon manure should be put down first to alleviate any nitrogen robbery by the sawdust. Some gardeners have experimented with mushroom compost and redwood sawdust. Others have used shredded pine bark or cocoa bean hull not more than two inches in depth. Put the mulch on after the soil has warmed up in the spring and keep it piled high during the growing season.

Gardeners have found that a well mulched bush doesn't invite predators. A good thick mulch and adequate ventilation are also the best preventative for the old nemesis, black spot.

When winter finally rolls around, you can prevent winter injury of roses from heaving and thawing. A proper application of a good mulch around the plants prevents the soil from freezing too deep and acts as an insulator. You might like to try a four to five inch mulch of ground corn cobs, manure, straw or peat moss. Put it on in the fall after the ground has been partially frozen, or not later than December. If your roses have been mulched during the summer, simply add two or three inches more of mulch material. That will keep the soil temperature more constant and prevent damage. Some rose growers prefer to mound their plants with soil to a depth of six to eight inches, but this is hard work and unnecessary.

SHRUBBERY

Established shrubs, like most other plants, should receive a good mulch during the growing season. Strawy manure makes an excellent mulching material during the early summer months. A leaf mulch under most shrubs will also replenish organic matter in the soil. Unless fungus disease is a problem, leaves should be left where they fall and should be supplemented by liberal mulching with grass clippings, peat, corn cobs, straw, composted sawdust, or leaf mold. Leaves are an excellent mulch for shrubbery, and you might want to use it as a winter covering. Be sure to keep it well away from the trunk and apply only after the ground freezes to prevent the nesting of rodents.

INDEX

187

INDEX

188

INDEX

N

Nature and Properties of Soils, The, 18
Nebraska Crop Improvement Association, 21
Nematodes, Citrus, 45
Newspapers, 48, 109–114, 141, 163, 184
  ways to use, 109
New York City Commission of Air Resources, 102
Nitrogen, x, 11, 22, 26, 27, 30, 31, 59, 61, 75, 79, 119, 129, 130, 132, 140, 144, 157, 185
  deficiency, 127–128, 133
Nutrients, 9, 17, 22, 23, 26, 47, 62, 79, 176

O

Oats, 65, 128, 129
Ohio Department of Highways, 42
Ohio Edison Company, 71, 73
Okra, 152–153
Onions, 11, 153
Organic Gardening Experimental Farm, 83, 85, 157
Organic material, vii, 20–24, 26, 27, 29, 30, 32, 43, 56
Organic salts, 31
Oriental poppies, 181
Ornamentals, 171–186
Oxygen, 27
Oyster shell, 77

P

Pansy, 181
Papaya, 168
Paper, 10, 48, 49
Parsnip, 125, 153
Patterson, Pat, 150
Peaches, 85, 94, 95
Peanut shells, 75, 142
Peas, 125, 136, 154
Peat moss, 55, 74, 128, 149, 152, 161, 162, 164, 170, 175, 176, 179, 185, 186
Pennsylvania State Agricultural Experiment Station, 39
Peonies, 126, 142, 181

Peppers, 3, 125, 135, 136, 141, 154–155
Perennials, 50, 57, 72, 117–118, 119, 139, 177
Pesticides, x
pH, 14, 55, 62, 161
Phosphorous, 26, 27, 30
Picon, 75–76
Pierson, Joan, 146
Pine chips, 58–59, 70
Pine needles, 41, 50, 74, 127, 140, 157, 161, 162, 169, 171, 176, 177
Plant roots, x, 20, 29
Plastic mulch, 101–108, 158
  drawbacks, viii, 101
  Ruth Stout on, 103–108
  toxic fumes from, 102
Podzolic, 14
Poinsettias, 181
Polscer, Kenneth, 158
Potash, 26, 62, 75, 119
Potassium, 27
Potatoes, 4, 11, 70, 155–158
Public Works, 43
Pumpkins, 158

R

Radishes, 158–159
Raspberries, 44, 47–48, 49, 57, 168–169
Rawson, Harold, 7–9
Raymond, Dexter, 151
Rhododendrons, 142, 182
Rhubarb, 54, 57, 89, 159
Rice hulls, 75, 128
Rodale, J.I., 84, 94, 98, 99
Rodale, Robert, 97–99
Root zone, 9
Rosen, H.P., 182
Roses, 9, 50, 72, 77, 89, 139, 143, 176, 182–185
Rot, 152
  brown, 45
  crown, 45, 119
  fruit, 45
  root, 26, 45
Rotation, 21, 27
Ruth Stout No-Work Garden Book, The, 43

INDEX

Virgil, 83
Voigt, Owen M., 77–81

W

Wandzell, Bob, 53
Ward, Vernon, 125
Watermelon, 150, 170–171
Watson, E.M., 150
Wood, Margaret L., 85–90
Wood chips, 13, 44–45, 48, 49, 69–74, 143, 152, 168, 169, 170

Wright, Pearl, 178
Wright University, 182
Williamson, Cynthia, 135–136

Y

Yearbook of Agriculture, 15

Z

Zinc, 27
Zinnias, 127